CICERO
PRO LEGE MANILIA

An Edition for Schools
prepared by
Mary S. R. Burns
Henry L. Philip
William F. Ritchie
Kenneth G. Silver
as a follow-up reader to
Ecce Romani

By permission of the
Scottish Classics Group

Oliver & Boyd

Oliver & Boyd
Robert Stevenson House
1–3 Baxter's Place
Leith Walk
Edinburgh EH1 3BB
A Division of Longman Group Limited

ISBN 0 05 003259 3

First published 1980

Set in 11/12 pt and 9/11 pt Baskerville 169

Printed in Great Britain by
McCorquodale (Newton) Ltd
Newton le Willows, Merseyside

CONTENTS

ACKNOWLEDGMENTS

The editors and publishers are grateful to the following for supplying and giving permission for the reproduction of photographs: The Mansell Collection, front cover and p. 11; The Trustees of the British Museum, p. 27.

The illustrations on pp. 9, 25 and 44–5 are by Iain McIntosh, and that on p. 29 is by Hamish Gordon.

INTRODUCTION

The speech, Pro Lege Manilia, was delivered before the Roman people in 66 B.C.

Since 92 B.C. Mithridates VI of Pontus had been conducting a continuous campaign of harassment against the Romans. A succession of outstanding generals, including such great figures as Sulla and Lucullus, had been sent to deal with him. They had won notable victories over him, but Mithridates himself had always evaded capture and after each defeat he would lie low long enough to repair his shattered fortunes before resuming his attack on Roman interests. The inhabitants of the provinces in Asia Minor, particularly the province of Asia, were happy to support him, for their wealth had made them vulnerable to the greed of the Roman governors and tax-collectors, and Mithridates offered them the opportunity of revenge.

Gnaeus Pompeius, born in the same year as Cicero (106 B.C.), had already gained the reputation of an outstandingly successful leader. The annihilation of the remnants of Marius' supporters in 81 B.C., the victory over Lepidus at Mutina in 77 B.C. and his claim to have ended the Slave War in 71 B.C. had made him an obvious choice when the Romans decided in 67 B.C. to appoint a supreme commander to eliminate the menace of the pirates who had for so long hampered Roman trade and communication over most of the Mediterranean. That command, conferred upon him by the Lex Gabinia, was executed with such zeal, efficiency and success that he utterly eclipsed the renown of any other general. Even his presence in Asia, where he lingered after the defeat of the dreaded pirates, excited awe among all who were aware of it.

It was at this point that Mithridates decided to launch a new offensive against the Romans in Asia Minor. The tribune Manilius therefore proposed a law to hand over the command against Mithridates to Pompey, and the opportunity to support the law was eagerly seized by Cicero, who was a very great admirer of Pompey. The speech which follows is an eloquent tribute to a remarkable soldier, and its wide-ranging references to men and affairs provide a conspectus of Roman political life which is simultaneously interesting, informative and stylistically satisfying.

M. TULLI CICERONIS
DE IMPERIO CN. POMPEI
AD QUIRITES ORATIO

N.B. In the notes we have used the following convention when quoting from the Latin: where six dots are used, the note deals with the Latin words omitted as well as with those quoted; where three dots are used, the note deals only with the Latin words quoted.

1 **in hac ...... dicendi**: This is all one phrase. **mihi** is closely linked with **insolita** – *unusual for me*.

Quirites: *citizens of Rome*, a more dignified form of address than **cives**. The word appeals to their sense of tradition. Romulus, the founder of Rome, was given the title Quirinus after his death.

5 **non tam ... quam**: *not so much ... as*.

9 **vectigalibus**: The word **vectigalia** is used not only of the taxes paid to Rome by her subjects in the provinces but also, as here, of *the states which pay taxes*.

10 **Tigrane**: Tigranes was king of Armenia and son-in-law of Mithridates, for whom he provided a refuge in Armenia when he was trying to escape capture by the Romans.

ad occupandam Asiam: *to seize Asia*.

11 **equitibus Romanis**: *Roman knights*. This was the class in Roman society to which those engaged in business and commerce belonged. They were wealthy and therefore influential in the state.

13 **res**: *fortunes, sums of money*.

aguntur: *are at stake*.

in vestris vectigalibus exercendis: *in farming your taxes*. See page 43 for details of the tax system.

14 **qui**: This refers to the **equites** mentioned in line 11.

15 **Bithyniae**: See map on page 9. At the time when the conflict between Mithridates and the Romans began, the king of Bithynia was 'an ally and friend of the Roman people', (see page 10, line 9); but on his death in 75/74 B.C. he bequeathed his kingdom to Rome and it became a Roman province.

16 **vicos exustos esse**: Cicero now gives details of the information which has reached him about the situation in Asia Minor. Each piece of information is therefore expressed in the Accusative and Infinitive.

17 **Ariobarzanis**: Ariobarzanes was king of Cappadocia. (See map.)

18 **Lucullum**: Lucius Lucullus was sent in 74 B.C. to carry on the campaign against Mithridates.

19 **huic qui successerit**: *his successor*, Manius Acilius Glabrio.

22 **praeterea neminem**: *and he alone* (literally *and no one else besides*). This phrase must be taken closely with **eundem hunc unum**.

Cicero congratulates himself on having such an excellent theme: the character of Gnaeus Pompeius and his suitability for the war in Asia, where the situation is now critical. He identifies three main points to be considered.

in hac insolita mihi ratione dicendi, Quirites, causa talis
oblata est in qua oratio deesse nemini possit.   dicendum est
enim de Cn. Pompei singulari eximiaque virtute.   huius
autem orationis difficilius est exitum quam principium
5   invenire.   ita mihi non tam copia quam modus in dicendo
quaerendus est.
    atque ut inde oratio mea proficiscatur unde haec omnis
causa ducitur, bellum grave et periculosum vestris
vectigalibus ac sociis a duobus potentissimis regibus infertur,
10   Mithridate et Tigrane, qui occasionem sibi ad occupandam
Asiam oblatam esse arbitrantur.   equitibus Romanis,
honestissimis viris, adferuntur ex Asia cotidie litterae,
quorum magnae res aguntur in vestris vectigalibus exercendis
occupatae;   qui ad me causam rei publicae periculaque
15   suarum rerum detulerunt: Bithyniae, quae nunc vestra
provincia est, vicos exustos esse complures;   regnum
Ariobarzanis, quod finitimum est vestris vectigalibus, totum
esse in hostium potestate;   L. Lucullum magnis rebus gestis
ab eo bello discedere;   huic qui successerit, non satis esse
20   paratum ad tantum bellum administrandum;   unum ab
omnibus sociis et civibus ad id bellum imperatorem deposci
et expeti, eundem hunc unum ab hostibus metui, praeterea
neminem.

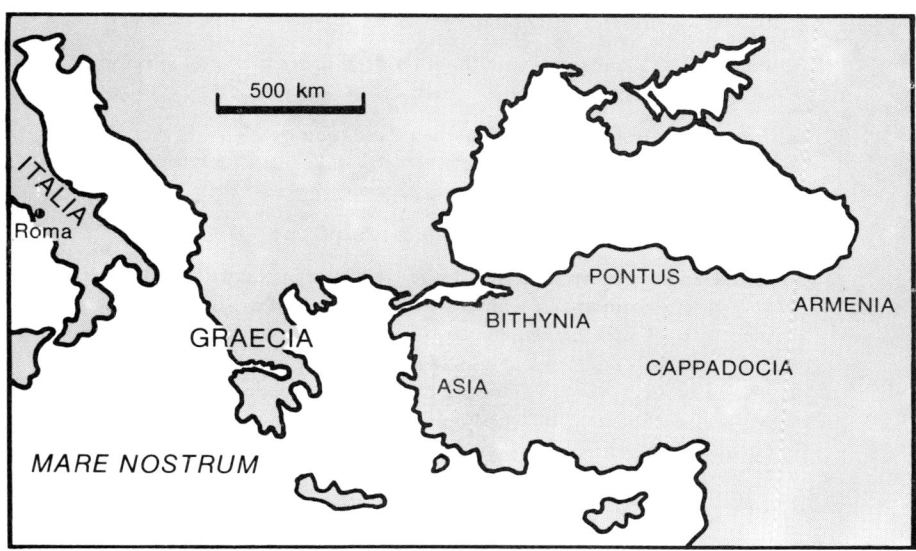

5   **genus . . . . . . quod**: *the nature of the war is such that.*

6   **ad persequendi studium**: It is common in Latin to find a genitive between a preposition and a noun governed by the preposition.

7   **cum . . . tum**: *both . . . and, not only . . . but also.*

9   **sociorum atque amicorum (populi Romani)**. This phrase denotes a relationship between Rome and another state whereby Rome guaranteed protection to the state concerned, but the state remained autonomous.

12   **quibus est . . . consulendum**: *whose interests must be consulted.* When used with the dative case, **consulere** means *to consult the interests of.* With the accusative case, it means *to ask the advice of.*
       et ipsorum et rei publicae causa: *both for their own sakes and for the sake of the state.* Note the position of **causa**.

14   **praeter** (+acc.): *to a greater degree (than).*

15   **Mithridatico bello superiore**: *in the previous war against Mithridates.*

16   **uno die . . . . . . litterarum**: Note the build-up of effect produced by **uno . . . tota . . . tot . . . uno . . . una . . .**
       tota in Asia: Note the position of **in** between adjective and noun.

18   **necandos trucidandosque denotavit**: *marked down as people to be killed and massacred.* This massacre of Roman citizens had taken place in Asia in 88 B.C. at Mithridates' instigation. About 80,000 died.

19   **poenam . . . . . . scelere**: Note the interlaced order of words, a common stylistic device in Latin.

20   **annum . . . . . . regnat**: In Latin, when a situation which has existed in the past continues in the present, the present tense is used. This is translated in English in the form *something has been happening for some time.*

21   **ita . . . ut**: *in such a way that.* **ita** leads us to expect **ut**.

23   **triumphavit . . . triumphavit**: This is an example of the figure of speech known as Anaphora, in which a word is repeated at the beginning of successive clauses or sentences to produce emphasis. Note that **de Mithridate** has to be taken with both clauses.
       L. Sulla: Sulla, like Lucullus, had campaigned successfully against Mithridates and in 83 B.C. had been awarded a triumph, the right to lead his troops in procession through Rome to celebrate a victorious campaign and to offer thanks to the gods.
       L. Murena: He too celebrated a triumph over Mithridates (81 B.C.).

causa quae sit, videtis.   nunc quid agendum sit, considerate.   primum mihi videtur de genere belli, deinde de magnitudine, tum de imperatore deligendo esse dicendum.

I. *The nature of the war and its harmful effect on (a) the glory of Rome, (b) her allies and (c) her revenues.*

5 genus est eius belli quod maxime vestros animos excitare atque inflammare ad persequendi studium debeat; in quo agitur populi Romani gloria quae vobis a maioribus cum magna in omnibus rebus, tum summa in re militari tradita est; agitur salus sociorum atque amicorum, pro qua maiores
10 vestri magna et gravia bella gesserunt; aguntur certissima populi Romani vectigalia et maxima; aguntur bona multorum civium, quibus est a vobis et ipsorum et rei publicae causa consulendum.

Pompey

(a) The conduct of Mithridates has tarnished the glory of Rome. In spite of the successes of Rome's generals, Mithridates continues to flourish.

et quoniam semper appetentes gloriae praeter ceteras
15 gentes fuistis, delenda est vobis illa macula Mithridatico bello superiore concepta.   is enim qui uno die tota in Asia, tot in civitatibus, uno nuntio atque una significatione litterarum cives Romanos necandos trucidandosque denotavit, non modo adhuc poenam nullam suo dignam scelere suscepit, sed
20 ab illo tempore annum iam tertium et vicesimum regnat.
etenim adhuc ita cum illo rege contenderunt imperatores nostri ut ab illo insignia victoriae, non victoriam reportarent.   triumphavit L. Sulla, triumphavit L. Murena de Mithridate, duo fortissimi viri et summi imperatores;

1 **triumpharunt**: This is a shortened form of **triumphaverunt**. In verbs which have **-v-** in the perfect stem, the **-v-** and the vowel which follows it are sometimes dropped.
pulsus: *though beaten.*

2 **laus . . . . . . quod**: *praise must be ascribed for what* . . . This phrase is balanced by **venia danda quod**.

4 **Sullam . . . res publica, Murenam Sulla**: Note the balance, a clue to the fact that **ab eo bello**, **in Italiam** and **revocavit** must be taken with both parts of the clause.
res publica: *the political situation.*

8 **aedificasset**: See note on **triumpharunt** (line 1).

10 **simularet**: Note the change of tense from pluperfect to imperfect subjunctive.

11 **ad eos duces**: This refers to an anti-Roman group in Spain. A Roman called Sertorius was leading the Spaniards in a war against Rome.

14 **ancipiti contentione districti**: *torn by a struggle on two fronts*, i.e. the war in the East against Mithridates, and the war in Spain against Sertorius.

16 **Sertorianae atque Hispaniensis**: These adjectives explain to which war **alterius partis** refers.

18 **ita . . . ut**: Compare the note on page 10, line 21.
Note the two sets of balanced phrases in the **ut** clause:
(a) the subjects are balanced (i) **initia illa rerum gestarum**
                          (ii) **haec quae nuper acciderunt**
(b) the datives are balanced   (i) **non felicitati sed virtuti**
                          (ii) **non culpae sed fortunae**
The phrase **tribuenda esse videantur** has to be taken with both parts of the clause, i.e. with each subject and each pair of datives. **videantur** literally means *seem*. Translate *it seems that.*

20 **haec autem quae**: *whereas these events which.*

23 **videte . . . . . . putetis**: *consider what attitude you think you should adopt.*

25 **iniuriosius**: *rather harshly* (a comparative adverb).

27 **quo tandem animo**: *what, tell me, ought your attitude to be?* **tandem** is used in a question to which the answer is obvious – a rhetorical question.

28 **legati quod**: **legati** is the subject of the **quod** clause and is placed first for emphasis.

29 **Corinthum . . . . . . exstinctum esse**: The destruction of Corinth in 146 B.C. was an example of the ruthless way in which Rome eliminated all rivals, real or imagined, in order to achieve Mediterranean supremacy. Corinth had for centuries played a leading part in the political, economic and artistic life of Greece. Her destruction, according to Cicero, was like the sudden extinction of a very bright light.

sed ita triumpharunt ut ille pulsus superatusque regnaret. verum tamen illis imperatoribus laus est tribuenda quod egerunt, venia danda quod reliquerunt, propterea quod ab eo bello Sullam in Italiam res publica, Murenam Sulla
5   revocavit.
    Mithridates autem omne reliquum tempus non ad oblivionem veteris belli, sed ad comparationem novi contulit. qui postea, cum maximas aedificasset ornassetque classes exercitusque permagnos comparasset et se Bosporanis
10 bellum inferre simularet, usque in Hispaniam legatos ac litteras misit ad eos duces quibuscum tum bellum gerebamus. hoc fecit ut, cum duobus in locis disiunctissimis uno consilio a binis hostium copiis bellum terra marique gereretur, vos ancipiti contentione districti de imperio
15 dimicaretis.
    sed tamen alterius partis periculum, Sertorianae atque Hispaniensis, Cn. Pompei divino consilio ac singulari virtute depulsum est. in altera parte ita res a L. Lucullo, summo viro, est administrata ut initia illa rerum gestarum non
20 felicitati eius sed virtuti, haec autem, quae nuper acciderunt, non culpae sed fortunae tribuenda esse videantur. sed de Lucullo dicam alio loco. de vestri autem imperii dignitate atque gloria, quoniam is est exorsus orationis meae, videte quem animum suscipiendum putetis.

(b) *In the past, Roman pride would not have tolerated such insolence. Rome's allies and friends are now clamouring for the strong personal leadership of Pompey.*

25   maiores nostri saepe, mercatoribus nostris iniuriosius tractatis, bella gesserunt. vos, tot milibus civium Romanorum uno nuntio atque uno tempore necatis, quo tandem animo esse debetis? legati quod erant appellati superbius, Corinthum patres vestri totius Graeciae lumen
30 exstinctum esse voluerunt. vos eum regem inultum esse

1   **consularem**: Once a man had held the consulship, he ranked as **consularis**, a status of special privilege and precedence. Mithridates' offence was all the greater in that he had killed an ambassador of such importance.

5   **quid?**: *then again.* A new point is about to be made.
      quod: *the fact that.* The **quod** clause is the object of **ferre**.

13   **summa**: *the highest qualities.*
      propter: *near at hand* (here used adverbially).

14   **quo ...... aegrius**: *and so they miss him all the more keenly.*

15   **tanta**: *of such a size.*

16   **iis**: Take with **contenti**. (**iis** refers to **vectigalia**.)

17   **et ... et ... et ... et ...**: A series of balanced phrases, each containing an ablative and a genitive. Note how effective it is to keep the longest phrase (**multitudine ...... exportantur**) to the end.

26   **pecuaria**: This refers to *cattle farming*, as opposed to *arable farming* (**agri cultura**) and *merchant shipping* (**mercatorum navigatio**). In the next sentence Cicero mentions three forms of taxes raised by the state from those three sources:
      (a) duties on imports and exports at harbours (**portoria**);
      (b) a land-tax or tithe (**decuma = decima pars**), calculated according to the annual yield of the province;
      (c) rental from the **ager publicus**. Those who rented the land paid duty on the number of cattle grazed. This grazing-tax (**scriptura**) was levied according to a registered list.

29   **totius ... uno ... uno ...**: The repetition of **uno** emphasises how easily a whole year's work could be lost.

32   **exercent atque exigunt**: The **equites** employed **publicani** to administer (**exercent**) the tax system. The **publicani** sometimes employed subcontractors (**familiae**) to make the actual collection (**exigunt**).

33   **cum una excursio**: Note that this **cum** clause and the one beginning **cum publicani** also depend on the initial question (**quo tandem animo ...**).

35   **magno periculo se habere arbitrentur**: *They think that they* (**se**) *are maintaining at great risk.*

36   **fructui sunt**: *are profitable* (Predicative Dative).

37   **conservaritis**: a shortened form of **conservaveritis**.

patiemini, qui legatum populi Romani consularem vinculis
ac verberibus excruciatum necavit? illi libertatem
imminutam civium Romanorum non tulerunt. vos ereptam
vitam neglegetis?
5 quid? quod salus sociorum summum in periculum ac
discrimen vocatur, quo tandem animo ferre debetis? regno
est expulsus Ariobarzanes rex, socius populi Romani atque
amicus. imminent duo reges toti Asiae non solum vobis
inimicissimi, sed etiam vestris sociis atque amicis. civitates
10 autem omnes cunctae Asiae atque Graeciae vestrum
auxilium exspectare propter periculi magnitudinem
coguntur. vident et sentiunt hoc idem quod vos, unum
virum esse in quo summa sint omnia, et eum propter esse,
quo etiam carent aegrius.

(c) *Even the threat of war can be enough to discourage the trade and
business from which taxes are raised. Rome's economy will suffer unless
the provinces in Asia are protected.*

15 ceterarum provinciarum vectigalia, Quirites, tanta sunt ut
iis ad ipsas provincias tutandas vix contenti esse possimus;
Asia vero tam opima est ac fertilis ut et ubertate agrorum et
varietate fructuum et magnitudine pastionis et multitudine
earum rerum quae exportantur facile omnibus terris
20 antecellat. itaque haec vobis provincia, Quirites, non modo
a calamitate sed etiam a metu calamitatis est defendenda.
nam in ceteris rebus cum venit calamitas, tum detrimentum
accipitur. at in vectigalibus non solum adventus mali sed
etiam metus ipse adfert calamitatem. nam cum hostium
25 copiae non longe absunt, etiamsi irruptio nulla facta est,
tamen pecuaria relinquitur, agri cultura deseritur,
mercatorum navigatio conquiescit. ita neque ex portu
neque ex decumis neque ex scriptura vectigal conservari
potest. quare saepe totius anni fructus uno rumore periculi
30 atque uno belli terrore amittitur. quo tandem animo esse
existimatis aut eos qui vectigalia nobis pensitant aut eos qui
exercent atque exigunt, cum duo reges cum maximis copiis
propter adsint? cum una excursio equitatus perbrevi
tempore totius anni vectigal auferre possit? cum publicani
35 familias maximas magno periculo se habere arbitrentur?
putatisne vos illis rebus frui posse, nisi eos qui vobis fructui
sunt conservaritis, non solum calamitate sed etiam
calamitatis formidine liberatos?

1   **multi**: subject of **possunt**.

2   **ut non**: *without* (cf. line 6)

4   **id quod ipsi videtis**: *and this is something you can see for yourselves.*
      haec fides atque haec ratio pecuniarum: *our system of credit and finance.*

5   **in foro versatur**: *exists in the Forum.* The bankers' offices stood in the Forum; hence it is referred to as the money market. (Compare Wall Street in New York and Lombard Street in London in modern times.)
      implicata est ... et cohaeret: *is inextricably bound up with.* Two verbs of similar meaning are here used to emphasise one idea.

6   **illa ... haec**: **illa** refers to **pecuniis Asiaticis**, **haec** to what is present and visible, i.e. the money market in the Forum to which Cicero would point as he said **haec**.

10   **coniunctae cum re publica**: *which are closely linked with (the interests of) the state.*

16   **tantum laudis ... quantum**: *as much praise as.*
      forti viro et sapienti homini et magno imperatori: Note the triple grouping. Cicero likes to group words, phrases and clauses in threes ('pompous triads'), especially when he is building up to a climax.

17   **eius adventu**: *at the time of his arrival.*

19   **urbem Asiae clarissimam**: This refers to Cyzicus.

20   **quam**: *but ... it.*
      virtute, assiduitate, consilio: another triple grouping.

21   **ab eodem imperatore**: From this point to the end of the paragraph the clauses are all Accusative and Infinitive, depending on **dico** (line 17).

24   **quibus in oppidis**: *towns in which.* Note the difference between English and Latin idiom.

26   **aditu adventuque**: another example of two words conveying the same idea. (cf. line 5).
      spoliatum: *stripped of his possessions.*
      se ... supplicem contulisse: *he went as a suppliant.*

27   **salvis ...... vectigalibus**: *without injury to the allies of the Roman people and without loss of revenue.*

33   **Medea illa**: *the famous Medea.* Medea, daughter of King Aeetes, helped Jason to gain the Golden Fleece and then fled with him taking her younger brother with her. She killed her brother and scattered his limbs over the sea so that her father had to slow down his pursuit to collect them.
      illam praedicant: *people say that she.*

35   **eorum collectio dispersa**: *the collection of the scattered remains.*

non enim possunt una in civitate multi rem ac fortunas
amittere ut non plures secum in eandem trahant
calamitatem.   a quo periculo prohibete rem publicam; et,
mihi credite, id quod ipsi videtis, haec fides atque haec ratio
5   pecuniarum, quae Romae in foro versatur, implicata est cum
illis pecuniis Asiaticis et cohaeret.   ruere illa non possunt ut
haec non eodem labefacta motu concidant.   quare videte
num dubitandum vobis sit omni studio ad id bellum
incumbere, in quo gloria nominis vestri, salus sociorum,
10   vectigalia maxima, fortunae plurimorum civium coniunctae
cum re publica defendantur.

II.   *The scale of the war. Lucullus has already demonstrated how
much a good general can achieve; but Mithridates, displaying a
cunning as great as that of the legendary Medea, continues to outwit
our army.*

quoniam de genere belli dixi, nunc de magnitudine pauca
dicam.   potest enim hoc dici, belli genus esse ita necessarium
ut sit gerendum, non esse ita magnum ut sit
15   pertimescendum.   atque ut omnes intellegant me L. Lucullo
tantum impertire laudis quantum forti viro et sapienti
homini et magno imperatori debeatur, dico eius adventu
maximas Mithridatis copias omnibus rebus ornatas atque
instructas fuisse, urbemque Asiae clarissimam ab ipso rege
20   obsessam esse, quam L. Lucullus virtute, assiduitate, consilio
summis obsidionis periculis liberavit; ab eodem imperatore
classem magnam superatam esse atque depressam; magnas
hostium praeterea copias multis proeliis esse deletas;
Sinopen atque Amisum, quibus in oppidis erant domicilia
25   regis, ceterasque urbes Ponti et Cappadociae permultas uno
aditu adventuque esse captas; regem spoliatum ad alios se
reges supplicem contulisse; atque haec omnia salvis populi
Romani sociis atque integris vectigalibus esse gesta.
requiretur fortasse nunc quemadmodum, cum haec sint,
30   reliquum possit magnum esse bellum.   cognoscite,
Quirites!   non enim hoc sine causa quaeri videtur.
primum ex suo regno sic Mithridates profugit ut ex eodem
Ponto Medea illa quondam profugisse dicitur: illam
praedicant in fuga fratris sui membra, in iis locis qua se parens
35   persequeretur, dissipavisse ut eorum collectio dispersa

17

2   **vim auri**:   *quantity of gold.*

4   **diligentius**:   The use of the comparative implies criticism.

5   **illum ... hos**:   **illum** refers to Aeetes, **hos** to the Romans.

     ita illum ...... tardavit: In balanced phrases and clauses, words common to both parts do not normally appear twice:

       ita illum in persequendi studio maeror (tardavit)

         hos (in persequendi studio) laetitia tardavit.

     (cf. page 12, line 18)

7   **in illo timore et fuga**:   literally *in that terror and flight.* It is probably better to combine the two nouns into *in that panic-stricken flight.* This figure of speech, called Hendiadys, is common in Latin.

8   **diffidentem ... afflictum ... perditum**:   These all refer to **hunc.** Translate **diffidentem** *when he lacked confidence.*

15   **fani ... diripiendi causa**:   *to plunder a ... shrine.*

      fani ...... adductum: The Accusative and Infinitive in this clause explains what the **opinio** was.

18   **urbem**:   *one city.*

19   **proeliis usus erat secundis**:   *had enjoyed successes in battle.*

20   **desiderio suorum**:   *by a longing for their own people.*

24   **tantum ... quantum**:   *as much ... as* (cf. page 16, line 16).

      victus ... incolumis: *when defeated ... when unbeaten.*

25   **numquam est ausus optare**:   *he would never have dared to pray for.*

26   **non fuit eo contentus quod ...**:   *he was not content with what ...* He had not expected to reach his homeland after being beaten.

32   **hic**:   *at this point.*

33   **mederi potuisset**:   *could have remedied.*

35   **stipendiis confectis erant**:   *had completed their service.*

36   **vos coniectura perspicite**:   *you must imagine them for yourselves.* The rest of the sentence (**quantum ...... pulso**) summarises the points which Cicero has decided not to detail.

37   **factum**:   *has become.*

      quod coniungant: *which (they) join in waging.*

maerorque patrius celeritatem persequendi retardaret. sic
Mithridates fugiens maximam vim auri atque argenti
pulcherrimarumque rerum omnium in Ponto reliquit. haec
dum nostri colligunt omnia diligentius, rex ipse e manibus
5 effugit. ita illum in persequendi studio maeror, hos laetitia
tardavit.

Our forces are further hampered by adverse propaganda, and the
seriousness of the situation is aggravated, on the one hand, by the
growth of Mithridates' support and, on the other, by the partial
disbandment of Roman forces.

hunc in illo timore et fuga Tigranes, rex Armenius, excepit
diffidentemque rebus suis confirmavit et afflictum erexit
perditumque recreavit. cuius in regnum posteaquam L.
10 Lucullus cum exercitu venit, plures etiam gentes contra
imperatorem nostrum concitatae sunt. erat enim metus
iniectus iis nationibus quas numquam populus Romanus
lacessendas bello putavit. erat etiam alia gravis atque
vehemens opinio quae animos gentium barbararum
15 pervaserat, fani locupletissimi et religiosissimi diripiendi
causa in eas oras nostrum esse exercitum adductum. ita
nationes multae atque magnae novo quodam terrore ac metu
concitabantur. noster autem exercitus, tametsi urbem ex
Tigranis regno ceperat et proeliis usus erat secundis, tamen
20 nimia longinquitate locorum ac desiderio suorum
commovebatur.
Mithridates autem et suam manum iam confirmarat et
magnis adventiciis auxiliis multorum regum et nationum
iuvabatur. itaque tantum victus efficere potuit quantum
25 incolumis numquam est ausus optare. nam cum se in
regnum suum recepisset, non fuit eo contentus quod ei
praeter spem acciderat, sed in exercitum nostrum clarum
atque victorem impetum fecit. sinite me hoc loco, Quirites,
praeterire nostram calamitatem quae tanta fuit ut eam ad
30 aures imperatoris non ex proelio nuntius sed ex sermone
rumor adferret.
hic in illa gravissima belli offensione L. Lucullus, qui
tamen aliqua ex parte iis incommodis mederi fortasse
potuisset, vestro iussu coactus, partem militum, qui iam
35 stipendiis confectis erant, dimisit, partem M'. Glabrioni
tradidit. multa praetereo consulto; sed vos coniectura
perspicite quantum illud bellum factum putetis, quod
coniungant reges potentissimi, renovent agitatae nationes,

1 **integrae gentes**: *countries not previously involved.*
   novus imperator: i.e. Glabrio. (See page 8, line 19)

8 **quem potissimum ...**: This clause explains the preceding **haec**.

10 **unus qui**: *the only man who.*
    hominum qui nunc sunt: *men of today.* Cicero balances this personal
    phrase with the abstract expression **antiquitatis memoriam**, *the memory
    of the past*, i.e. *the recorded achievements of our predecessors.*

11 **virtute**: *in merit.*

12 **cuiusquam animum ... dubium facere**: *to raise doubts in anyone's mind.*

14 **quattuor has res**: *these four qualities.*

16 **esse debuit**: *ought to have been.* In Cicero's opinion, Pompey was bound to
    be more knowledgeable because he began learning the business of
    generalship when still very young.

17 **qui**: *for he.* There are several triple groupings in this paragraph.
    ad patris exercitum: His father, a distinguished general, was fighting
    Italian allies who had rebelled against Rome (c. 89 B.C.).

19 **extrema pueritia**: ablative expressing 'time when'. **pueritia** ended
    about the age of seventeen.

20 **ineunte adulescentia**: *at the start of his youth* (Ablative Absolute).
    adulescentia was the period between seventeen and thirty years of age.
    maximi ipse exercitus: At the age of 23 Pompey raised an army of his
    own to help the dictator Sulla. Greater emphasis is given to this phrase by
    placing **ipse** between **maximi** and **exercitus**.

21 **cum hoste ... cum inimico**: **hostis** is an enemy of the state, usually a
    foreigner, while **inimicus** is a personal enemy.

26 **stipendiis**: **stipendium**, the word originally used for a soldier's pay,
    came to mean also *a campaign*, because soldiers were normally paid only at
    the end of the fighting. (See page 18, line 35.)

28 **civile**: Pompey supported Sulla in the civil war against the followers of
    Marius (83 B.C.).
    Africanum: the campaign against Marius' supporters who had by this
    time fled to Africa (81 B.C.).
    Transalpinum: a war against Gallic tribes who were blocking Pompey's
    route to Spain (77 B.C.).
    Hispaniense: the war against Sertorius who was leading a revolt in Spain
    (76–72 B.C.). (Cf. also page 13, lines 10 and 17.)

29 **servile**: Crassus had already defeated Spartacus, the leader of the slave
    revolt in Italy (71 B.C.), but Pompey took all the credit by merely
    destroying the last remnants of Spartacus' army on his return from Spain.
    navale: The pirates had infested the Mediterranean and made trade
    virtually impossible. Pompey had defeated them in a naval campaign in
    67 B.C., the year preceding this speech.

suscipiant integrae gentes, novus imperator accipiat vetere exercitu pulso.

III. *The choice of general. Pompey possesses the four qualities which are essential in a good general.*

satis mihi multa verba fecisse videor quare esset hoc bellum genere ipso necessarium, magnitudine periculosum.   restat
5   ut de imperatore ad id bellum deligendo dicendum esse videatur.   utinam, Quirites, virorum fortium atque innocentium copiam tantam haberetis ut haec vobis deliberatio difficilis esset, quem potissimum tantis rebus ac tanto bello praeficiendum putaretis!   nunc vero cum sit
10   unus Cn. Pompeius qui non modo gloriam hominum qui nunc sunt, sed etiam antiquitatis memoriam virtute superarit, quae res est quae cuiusquam animum in hac causa dubium facere possit?   ego enim sic existimo in summo imperatore quattuor has res inesse oportere, scientiam rei militaris,
15   virtutem, auctoritatem, felicitatem.

(*a*) **scientia:** *His military skill, gained through first-hand experience, is unquestioned.*

quis igitur hoc homine scientior umquam aut fuit aut esse debuit?   qui e ludo atque pueritiae disciplinis ad patris exercitum atque in militiae disciplinam profectus est; qui extrema pueritia miles in exercitu fuit summi imperatoris.
20   ineunte adulescentia maximi ipse exercitus imperator; qui saepius cum hoste conflixit quam quisquam cum inimico concertavit, plura bella gessit quam ceteri legerunt, plures provincias confecit quam alii concupiverunt; cuius adulescentia ad scientiam rei militaris non alienis praeceptis
25   sed suis imperiis, non offensionibus belli sed victoriis, non stipendiis sed triumphis est erudita.   quod denique genus esse belli potest in quo illum non exercuerit fortuna rei publicae?   civile, Africanum, Transalpinum, Hispaniense, servile, navale bellum, varia et diversa genera bellorum, non

1   **declarant**: The phrase **varia et diversa genera** sums up the list of wars with which the sentence begins and itself becomes the composite subject of **declarant**.

9   **tanta ...... quanta**: These words normally express the idea of one thing being 'as great as' another, i.e. equal. Here, however, the negative **non** produces a comparative meaning. Translate *these are greater in this one man than they were in all other generals*.

12   **testis**: The repetition of the word **testis** is a further example of Anaphora (cf. page 10, line 23).
      Italia: See page 20, line 28.

13   **Sicilia**: another phase in the war against Marius' supporters (82 B.C.).

15   **Africa ... Gallia ... Hispania**: See page 20, line 28.

21   **cum ... tum**: *both ... and*.

26   **hieme**: an ablative expressing 'time'. Roman sailors did not usually put to sea between November and March.

28   **arbitraretur**: *would have thought*. (The Potential Subjunctive introduces a supposition or possibility.)

31   **hosce**: Cicero is fond of this more emphatic form of *hos*.

33   **praesidio ... fuistis**: *you protected* (Predicative Dative). Note that the person to whom protection is given (**cui**) is also in the dative.
      classibus vestris: *with your fleets* (ablative case).

36   **longinqua**: *distant*, referring to foreign wars.
      fuit quondam: **fuit** here conveys the idea 'was, but is no longer'. The idea is reinforced by the repetition of **fuit**.

solum gesta ab hoc uno sed etiam confecta, declarant nullam rem esse in usu positam militari, quae huius viri scientiam fugere possit.

(*b*) **virtus**: *Many different qualities contribute to his all-round ability. The success of all his former campaigns bears witness to his swift and effective action in many different theatres of war.*

iam vero virtuti Cn. Pompei quae potest oratio par
5   inveniri? quid est quod quisquam aut illo dignum aut vobis novum aut cuiquam inauditum possit adferre? neque enim illae sunt solae virtutes imperatoris quae vulgo existimantur, labor in negotiis, fortitudo in periculis, industria in agendo, celeritas in conficiendo, consilium in providendo, quae tanta
10   sunt in hoc uno quanta in omnibus reliquis imperatoribus non fuerunt.

testis est Italia, quam ille ipse victor L. Sulla huius hominis virtute et subsidio confessus est liberatam. testis est Sicilia, quam multis undique cinctam periculis consilii celeritate
15   explicavit. testis est Africa, quae magnis oppressa hostium copiis eorum ipsorum sanguine redundavit. testis est Gallia, per quam legionibus nostris iter in Hispaniam Gallorum internicione patefactum est. testis est Hispania, quae saepissime plurimos hostes ab hoc superatos prostratosque
20   conspexit. testes nunc vero iam omnes sunt orae atque omnes exterae gentes ac nationes, denique maria omnia cum universa, tum in singulis oris omnes sinus atque portus.

quis enim toto mari locus per hos annos aut tam firmum habuit praesidium ut tutus esset, aut tam fuit abditus ut
25   lateret? quis navigavit qui non se aut mortis aut servitutis periculo committeret, cum aut hieme aut referto praedonum mari navigaret? hoc tantum bellum, tam turpe, tam vetus, tam late divisum atque dispersum quis umquam arbitraretur aut ab omnibus imperatoribus uno anno aut omnibus annis
30   ab uno imperatore confici posse? quam provinciam tenuistis a praedonibus liberam per hosce annos? quod vectigal vobis tutum fuit? quem socium defendistis? cui praesidio classibus vestris fuistis? quam multas existimatis insulas esse desertas, quam multas sociorum urbes aut metu
35   relictas aut a praedonibus esse captas?

sed quid ego longinqua commemoro? fuit hoc quondam, fuit proprium populi Romani, longe a domo bellare et

3   **dicam**: *am I to say* (Deliberative Subjunctive: cf. **querar** in line 5).

   a Brundisio: Travellers to the East would usually sail from Brundisium to the west coast of Greece and continue their journey overland. The pirates had made even this short sea crossing (less than 150 km) too dangerous to attempt.

4   **qui**: *those (ambassadors) who.* **qui** is often used by itself meaning *those who*. In this example, the pronoun **eos** is understood and together with **captos** forms an Accusative and Infinitive depending on **querar**.

5   **querar**: *am I to complain?* (Deliberative Subjunctive).

7   **duodecim secures**: Cicero refers to an occasion when two praetors were captured by the pirates. (A consul had twelve lictors, a praetor six.) The symbols of authority (the axes) are used to denote the magistrates themselves. This figure of speech is called Metonymy. (Compare 'the crown' used in English to refer to the Queen.)

8   **quid ... querar**: *Why should I complain about ...* (cf. line 5.)

   Ostiense incommodum: *the disaster at Ostia.* The pirates had dared to sail into Ostia, the port of Rome at the mouth of the Tiber, about 23 km from the city.

9   **labem atque ignominiam**: *that blot and disgrace,* another example of Hendiadys. Translate *that shameful blot.*

10   **inspectantibus vobis**: *while you were looking on* (Ablative Absolute). Ostia was so near to Rome that the citizens could almost be described as eye-witnesses of the events there.

14   **ostium Tiberinum ... Oceani ostium**: The mouth of the Tiber is contrasted with the mouth of the (Atlantic) Ocean, i.e. the Straits of Gibraltar.

17   **haec ...... sint**: **haec** is the subject of the Indirect Question **qua celeritate gesta sint**, which depends on **quamquam videtis**.

19   **nondum ...... mari**: *before the normal sailing season.*

21   **frumentaria subsidia**: *the mainstays of our corn-supply.* Sicily, Africa and Sardinia supplied most of the grain for Rome's vast population.

23   **duas Hispanias**: Roman Spain was divided into two provinces.

   Galliam Transalpinam: *Gaul beyond the Alps,* roughly that part of southern France now called Provence.

24   **Illyrici maris**: the eastern coast of the Adriatic, the district of modern Yugoslavia known as Dalmatia.

25   **duo maria Italiae**: the Adriatic (east of Italy) and the Tyrrhenian Sea (west of Italy). Pompey delegated the clearing of these to lieutenants and tackled Cilicia himself, since it was one of the main pirate strongholds.

29   **ubique**: literally *everywhere.* Translate *wherever they were.*

propugnaculis imperii sociorum fortunas non sua tecta
defendere. sociis ego nostris mare per hos annos clausum
fuisse dicam, cum exercitus vestri numquam a Brundisio nisi
hieme summa transmiserint?   qui ad vos ab exteris
5 nationibus venirent, captos querar, cum legati populi
Romani redempti sint?   mercatoribus tutum mare non
fuisse dicam, cum duodecim secures in praedonum
potestatem pervenerint?   quid ego Ostiense incommodum *blot,*
atque illam labem atque ignominiam rei publicae querar, *disgrace*
10 cum prope inspectantibus vobis classis ea, cui consul populi
Romani praepositus esset, a praedonibus capta et oppressa
est?   pro di immortales!   tantamne unius hominis
incredibilis ac divina virtus tam brevi tempore lucem adferre
rei publicae potuit ut vos, qui modo ante ostium Tiberinum
15 classem hostium videbatis, nunc nullam intra Oceani ostium
praedonum navem esse audiatis?

The **fasces** were a bundle of rods carried
by the attendants (lictors) of senior magistrates. They symbolised the magistrates' authority to punish by flogging. Outside the city,
an axe was added to the rods since there, under military law, a magistrate could impose
the death penalty.

atque haec qua celeritate gesta sint, quamquam videtis,
tamen a me in dicendo praetereunda non sunt.   Cn.
Pompeius nondum tempestivo ad navigandum mari Siciliam
20 adiit, Africam exploravit, in Sardiniam cum classe venit
atque haec tria frumentaria subsidia rei publicae firmissimis
praesidiis classibusque munivit.   inde cum se in Italiam
recepisset, duas Hispanias et Galliam Transalpinam
praesidiis ac navibus confirmavit, itemque in oram Illyrici
25 maris et in omnem Graeciam naves misit; ita duo maria
Italiae maximis classibus firmissimisque praesidiis
adornavit; ipse autem ut Brundisio profectus est,
undequinquagesimo die totam ad imperium populi Romani
Ciliciam adiunxit.   omnes qui ubique praedones fuerunt,

2   **tantum ...... dispersum**: These three phrases, emphasising the difficulties of the war, balance and contrast with **extrema hieme ... ineunte vere ... media aestate**, which emphasise the speed with which he ended it. (Triple groupings: cf. page 16, line 16.)

5   **est haec ... virtus imperatoris**: *such is his ... skill as a commander.*

6   **ceterae**: His qualities (**virtutes**) other than military skill are now being mentioned.

7   **quantae atque quam multae sunt**: Cicero delays these words to create greater impact.

9   **huius ...... virtutis**: **huius** agrees with **virtutis**. The words **administrae comitesque** are normally used of persons, but here they are applied to qualities (**artes**). English might use verbs: *which assist and accompany this skill.*

10   **quanta innocentia**: This is the first of a list of descriptive ablatives. When **esse** is used with such phrases, 'have', 'possess' or 'be endowed with' will usually produce an acceptable translation: *what integrity generals ought to possess!* Cicero avers that Pompey, unlike many other Roman generals, did not use his position to acquire personal wealth by corrupt means.

13   **quae breviter qualia sint**: In this sentence **quae** is the object of **consideremus**. (For the position of **quae** compare other uses of 'linking qui' such as **quae ubi audivit**: *when he heard this.*) The words **qualia sint** explain **quae** more precisely. The literal meaning is *let us briefly consider these qualities* (**quae**) *what they are like*. English would tend to use an abstract noun like *nature*. Translate *let us briefly consider the nature of these qualities.*

15   **ex aliorum contentione**: *by comparison with the qualities of others.*
            ipsa per sese: *simply by themselves.*

17   **ullo in numero putare**: *regard with any respect.*

18   **centuriatus veneant atque venierint**: **centuriatus** means *the rank or position of centurion.* Here it is plural – *promotions to the rank of centurion.* Normally, soldiers were promoted to this rank on merit; but Cicero suggests that in some armies generals chose those who were prepared to pay for this promotion.
            Distinguish **veneo** from **venio**. The former is a compound of **eo**: **veneo** = *I go for sale*, i.e. *I am sold.* (Compare **ven-do** *I offer for sale, I sell.*)
            quid ...... cogitare: Understand **possumus putare** from the previous sentence. A literal translation might be *What great or noble (thought) can we suppose* (**putare**) *that this man thinks* (**cogitare**) *about the state?'*

20   **ex aerario**: The **aerarium** was the state treasury at Rome.

21   **propter cupiditatem provinciae**: *because of his passionate desire for provincial command.*

22   **in quaestu reliquerit**: *he left it invested* (for his own advantage).

23   **facit ut**: *indicates that.*

partim capti interfectique sunt, partim unius huius imperio se
dediderunt. ita tantum bellum, tam diuturnum, tam longe
lateque dispersum Cn. Pompeius extrema hieme apparavit,
ineunte vere suscepit, media aestate confecit.

Sheer ability in a commander is not enough. Other outstanding
qualities set Pompey apart from and above other generals.

5   est haec divina atque incredibilis virtus imperatoris.
quid? ceterae, quas paulo ante commemorare coeperam,
quantae atque quam multae sunt! non enim bellandi virtus
solum in summo ac perfecto imperatore quaerenda est, sed
multae sunt artes eximiae huius administrae comitesque
10   virtutis. ac primum quanta innocentia debent esse
imperatores! quanta deinde in omnibus rebus
temperantia! quanta fide, quanta facilitate, quanto
ingenio, quanta humanitate! quae breviter qualia sint in
Cn. Pompeio consideremus. summa enim omnia sunt,
15   Quirites, sed ea magis ex aliorum contentione quam ipsa per
sese cognosci atque intellegi possunt. quem enim
imperatorem possumus ullo in numero putare, cuius in
exercitu centuriatus veneant atque venierint? quid hunc
hominem magnum aut amplum de re publica cogitare, qui
20   pecuniam ex aerario depromptam ad bellum
administrandum aut propter cupiditatem provinciae
magistratibus diviserit aut propter avaritiam Romae in
quaestu reliquerit? vestra admurmuratio facit, Quirites, ut
agnoscere videamini qui haec fecerint. ego autem nomino

1   **2** obverse   reverse

  1 A **denarius** with the head of Pompey the Great. The inscrip-
     tion reads CNaeus MAGNUS IMPERATOR. (*enlarged*)

  2 This gold **aureus** was issued by Pompey to celebrate his victory
     in Africa. On the obverse are the head of Africa personified and
     Pompey's **agnomen** MAGNUS. The laurel wreath round the
     edge of the coin symbolises Pompey's triumph. On the reverse,
     Pompey rides in a **quadriga**, with his son riding on the nearest
     horse. Overhead flies a figure of Victory holding a wreath. The
     letters PRO COS (standing for **pro consule**) indicate his
     rank. (*enlarged*)

1   **nisi qui ante voluerit**: *except the man who has first shown willingness* ....

3   **quocumque ventum sit**: *wherever they have gone*. The impersonal passive (cf. **pugnatum est**) is especially common with verbs of motion.

4   **quis ignorat**: The Indirect Question **quantas calamitates ......** **ferant** depends on **quis ignorat**. The important facts are mentioned first to concentrate the audience's attention, and the inversion of the two clauses gives added emphasis. (cf. **nunc quid agendum sit, considerate** on page 11, line 1; and the position of **recordamini** in line 6 below.)

    itinera: Roman governors had become notorious for the demands (e.g. free lodging, lavish provisions and 'gifts') which they made on the local communities during their official tours (**itinera**).

5   **civium Romanorum**: Twenty-three years before this, the Italians had won Roman citizenship as a result of the Social War. As **civitates liberae** they should therefore have been exempt from the expense of billeting soldiers for the winter.

6   **recordamini**: *recall!* (an imperative, not an indicative).

7   **quid ... fieri existimetis**: *what you think happens.*

    utrum ...... deletas: The question being put to the audience is in two balanced parts. In full form it would read:

utrum plures arbitramini

      militum vestrorum   armis   hostium urbes   (esse deletas)

   an (plures arbitramini)

      (militum vestrorum) hibernis   sociorum civitates   esse deletas

In a war (**armis**) one expects destruction at the hands of the enemy. Under a greedy commander, it could be just as costly for a community to support a defending army wintering (**hibernis**) in its midst.

10   **hic**: *in the circumstances.*

     cuius: The antecedent is **hunc hominem**.

11   **non modo**: These words here stand for **non modo non**. The second **non** is normally omitted when **sed ne ... quidem** follows.

     manus: The *hand* refers to deliberate plundering, while the *foot-mark* suggests only incidental damage caused by an army on the march.

12   **cuiquam pacato**: *any non-combatant.*

14   **qua sit temperantia**: *what restraint he has shown.* (For this use of the ablative compare **quanta innocentia** on page 26, line 10.)

15   **illam tantam celeritatem**: *such speed as that.*

17   **eximia vis remigum**: *exceptional rowing by a picked crew.*

18   **venti aliqui novi**: *some freak winds.*

20   **non ... non ... non ... non denique**: **denique** brings to an end the list of temptations which failed to distract Pompey from his course.

neminem. quare irasci mihi nemo poterit, nisi qui ante de
se voluerit confiteri. itaque propter hanc avaritiam
imperatorum quantas calamitates, quocumque ventum sit,
nostri exercitus ferant, quis ignorat? itinera quae per hosce
5 annos in Italia per agros atque oppida civium Romanorum
nostri imperatores fecerint, recordamini. tum facilius
statuetis quid apud exteras nationes fieri existimetis. utrum
plures arbitramini per hosce annos militum vestrorum armis
hostium urbes an hibernis sociorum civitates esse deletas?
10 hic miramur hunc hominem tantum excellere ceteris, cuius
legiones sic in Asiam pervenerint ut non modo manus tanti
exercitus sed ne vestigium quidem cuiquam pacato nocuisse
dicatur?

age vero, ceteris in rebus qua ille sit temperantia,
15 considerate. unde illam tantam celeritatem et tam
incredibilem cursum inventum putatis? non enim illum
eximia vis remigum aut ars inaudita quaedam gubernandi
aut venti aliqui novi tam celeriter in ultimas terras
pertulerunt, sed eae res, quae ceteros remorari solent, non
20 retardarunt. non avaritia ab instituto cursu ad praedam
aliquam devocavit, non libido ad voluptatem, non nobilitas
urbis ad cognitionem, non denique labor ipse ad quietem.

1   **signa et tabulas**: Provincial governors often corruptly acquired works of art to decorate their homes.

2   **ea**: The demonstrative pronoun **ea** sums up all that has gone before, from **signa** to **arbitrantur**.
    sibi and **ille** both refer to Pompey.

5   **fuisse**: Note the emphatic position – *there really existed.*

6   **hac quondam continentia**: The adverb **quondam** is used almost like an adjective here – *former.*
    quod: *a fact which.*

8   **lucem**: *light* in the sense of *hope.*

10   **quam**: Latin uses **quam** with **malle** since the latter is a contraction of **magis velle**.

13   **multum ... valet**: *is of great importance.*
    nemini dubium est quin: *no one can doubt that.*

14   **ea re**: *in that respect* (i.e. as far as **auctoritas** is concerned).

15   **vehementer ... pertinere**: *that it is of vital importance.* This is an Indirect Statement which depends on **quis ignorat**. (For the position of **quis ignorat** compare page 28, line 4.)

21   **quo**: *that ... to it.*

22   **completis templis**: This refers only to the steps of the temples surrounding the Forum, not to their interiors. The vantage points were 'thronged' with spectators seeking a better view of the Rostra or Speakers' Platform (**hic locus**).

23   **unum Pompeium**: *Pompey alone.*

24   **ut plura non dicam**: *to cut a long story short.*

25   **quantum ...... valeat**: *how important this man's personal prestige is.* (For this use of **valere** compare line 13 above.)

27   **exempla sumantur**: Literally *let my examples be taken.* **sumantur** illustrates a common use of the present subjunctive.
    qui quo die: *on the day on which he.*

28   **tanta ... vilitas annonae ... quantam**: *such cheapness of corn ... as.* Excellent harvests, usually possible only in peacetime, are expected to produce cheap prices. Pompey's appointment in itself was sufficient to produce a sharp fall in the price of corn because it was confidently expected that peace would soon be restored.

29   **ex summa inopia**: *after a period of extreme shortage.*

30   **spe ac nomine**: **nomen** refers to Pompey's reputation and **spes** to the hopes that the Romans placed in him.

33   **amisissetis**: *you would have lost.*

postremo signa et tabulas Graecorum oppidorum, quae ceteri
tollenda esse arbitrantur, ea sibi ille ne visenda quidem
existimavit.   itaque omnes nunc in iis locis Cn. Pompeium
sicut aliquem non ex hac urbe missum, sed de caelo delapsum
5   intuentur.   nunc denique incipiunt credere fuisse homines
Romanos hac quondam continentia, quod iam nationibus
exteris incredibile videbatur.   nunc imperii vestri splendor
illis gentibus lucem adferre coepit.   nunc intellegunt non
sine causa maiores suos tum, cum ea temperantia magistratus
10   habebamus, servire populo Romano quam imperare aliis
maluisse.

(c) **auctoritas:** *Without a prestigious presence, a general will not
be wholly successful. Pompey is not lacking on that score. The very
name of Pompey was enough to influence the course of events, even when
he was not personally present.*

et quoniam auctoritas quoque in bellis administrandis
multum atque in imperio militari valet, certe nemini dubium
est quin ea re idem ille imperator plurimum possit.
15   vehementer autem pertinere ad bella administranda, quid
hostes, quid socii de imperatoribus nostris existiment, quis
ignorat?   quod igitur nomen umquam in orbe terrarum
clarius fuit?   cuius res gestae pares?   de quo homine vos, id
quod maxime facit auctoritatem, tanta et tam praeclara
20   iudicia fecistis?   an vero ullam usquam esse oram tam
desertam putatis quo non illius diei fama pervaserit, cum
universus populus Romanus referto foro completisque
omnibus templis, ex quibus hic locus conspici potest, unum
Cn. Pompeium imperatorem depoposcit?   itaque ut plura
25   non dicam neque aliorum exemplis confirmem quantum
huius auctoritas valeat in bello, ab eodem Cn. Pompeio
omnium rerum egregiarum exempla sumantur; qui quo die
a vobis maritimo bello praepositus est imperator, tanta
repente vilitas annonae ex summa inopia et caritate rei
30   frumentariae consecuta est unius hominis spe ac nomine,
quantam vix ex summa ubertate agrorum diuturna pax
efficere potuisset.
iam accepta in Ponto calamitate, amisissetis Asiam,
Quirites, nisi divinitus Cn. Pompeium ad eas regiones fortuna
35   populi Romani attulisset.   huius adventus et Mithridatem
victoria insolita inflammatum continuit et Tigranem magnis
copiis minantem Asiae retardavit.   et quisquam dubitabit

2 **Cretensium legati**: Crete was a pirate stronghold. Cicero suggests that it was Pompey's prestige which caused the Cretans, when they were on the point of surrender, to send their delegation (**legati**) all the way to Cilicia, where Pompey then was, rather than to the local Roman commander.

4 **eique**: This refers to Pompey.

5 **iste**: *that*, spoken here with a note of contempt.

10 **reliquum est**: Cicero now turns to the last of the four qualities required by a successful general. (See page 21, lines 14–15.)

11 **Maximo, Marcello, Scipioni, Mario**: four great Roman generals of the past. (See page 43 for further details.)

13 **saepius**: *repeatedly*. **imperia**: *military commands*.

14 **fuit ... quibusdam viris**: The dative case with **esse** is used in a possessive sense – *certain men had*.

15 **quaedam ... divinitus adiuncta fortuna**: *some sort of good luck, divinely bestowed*.

17 **hac ...... dicendi**: *I shall exercise restraint in what I say*.

19 **domi militiae**: *at home and abroad*, i.e. both as civilian magistrate and as military commander.
quantas res and **quanta felicitate** are both to be taken with **gesserit** – *what outstanding successes he achieved* and *how much good fortune he enjoyed*.

20 **eius semper voluntatibus**: The position of this phrase shows that it has to be taken with each of the four verbs depending on **ut**.

23 **hoc**: The Accusative and Infinitive which follows **dicam** explains *this* in detail. This is a common Ciceronian technique to direct the attention of the audience to the detailed statement which follows.

24 **tam ... qui**: *so ... that he*. The relative **qui** introduces a Result Clause.

25 **tot et tantas res ... quot et quantas**: *as many great favours as* (**tot ... quot**, *as many as*; **tantas ... quantas**, *as great as*).
tacitus: *even in the silence of his own thoughts*.

27 **quare cum ......**: This long sentence is easier to follow if attention is paid to the balanced clauses and phrases. The main thought of the sentence begins at **dubitatis**, but leading up to it there are two **cum** clauses:
(a) **cum bellum ...... administrandum**
(b) **cum ei ...... fortuna**
Each of these clauses has a balance within it:
in (a) **ita necessarium ut ...**
       ita magnum ut ...
in (b) the catalogue of qualities – **scientia**, **virtus**, **auctoritas**, **fortuna**.

31 **dubitatis quin hoc tantum boni ... conferatis**: *do you hesitate to apply this great advantage*.

quid virtute perfecturus sit, qui tantum auctoritate
perfecerit?   Cretensium legati, cum in eorum insula noster
imperator exercitusque esset, ad Cn. Pompeium in ultimas
prope terras venerunt eique se omnes Cretensium civitates
5   dedere velle dixerunt.   quid?   idem iste Mithridates nonne
legatum ad eundem Cn. Pompeium usque in Hispaniam
misit?   potestis igitur iam constituere, Quirites, quantum
apud illos reges, quantum apud exteras nationes valitura sit
haec auctoritas.

(*d*) **felicitas**: *Consistent good fortune in the past augurs well for
future success. Pompey's previous record indicates that he is one whom
good luck continuously attends.*

10   reliquum est ut de felicitate timide et pauca dicamus.
ego enim sic existimo Maximo, Marcello, Scipioni, Mario et
ceteris magnis imperatoribus non solum propter virtutem,
sed etiam propter fortunam saepius imperia mandata atque
exercitus esse commissos.   fuit enim profecto quibusdam
15   summis viris quaedam ad res magnas bene gerendas divinitus
adiuncta fortuna.   de huius autem hominis felicitate, de quo
nunc agimus, hac utar moderatione dicendi ne aut invisa dis
immortalibus oratio nostra aut ingrata esse videatur.   itaque
non sum praedicaturus quantas ille res domi militiae, terra
20   marique, quantaque felicitate gesserit, ut eius semper
voluntatibus non modo cives adsenserint, socii
obtemperarint, hostes oboedierint, sed etiam venti
tempestatesque obsecundarint.   hoc brevissime dicam,
neminem umquam tam impudentem fuisse, qui ab dis
25   immortalibus tot et tantas res tacitus auderet optare, quot et
quantas di immortales ad Cn. Pompeium detulerunt.

*Pompey should be the obvious choice under any circumstances. The fact
that he is on the spot, ready to take over, eliminates all doubt.*

quare cum bellum sit ita necessarium ut neglegi non possit,
ita magnum ut accuratissime sit administrandum, et cum ei
imperatorem praeficere possitis in quo sit eximia belli
30   scientia, singularis virtus, clarissima auctoritas, egregia
fortuna, dubitatis, Quirites, quin hoc tantum boni, quod
vobis ab dis immortalibus oblatum et datum est, in rem
publicam conservandam atque amplificandam conferatis?

1   **quodsi**: *but even if.*

3   **nunc**: *in the present circumstances.*
    haec quoque opportunitas: The three **ut** clauses explain *this further fortunate coincidence.*

5   **ab iis qui habent**: This refers to the existing commanders, Lucullus, Glabrio and Marcius Rex, who each had an army.

7   **at enim**: *but it will be pointed out that.* These words introduce an objection to what has been said.

8   **Catulus** and **Hortensius** feared that the proposals of Manilius to give Pompey special powers to deal with the crisis in the East were a threat to the republican constitution. Ever since the expulsion of the kings, the Romans had been unwilling to vest supreme power in one man.

9   **fortunae**: *wealth.*

10   **ab hac ratione dissentiunt**: *disagree with this proposal.*

11   **dignissimum esse Pompeium**: This Accusative and Infinitive depends on **ait** in the previous sentence.

12   **sed ... tamen**: *but in spite of all that.* **tamen** simply reinforces **sed**.

13   **ista oratio**: *that argument of yours.*
    re: *by the facts*, i.e. the appointment of Pompey as supreme commander against the pirates was a success.

17   **ex hoc ... loco**: i.e. the Rostra.

19   **si plus ... auctoritas tua ... valuisset, ... teneremus**: *if your influence had been stronger, would we possess ....* Note that an imperfect subjunctive in the main clause of a Conditional Sentence is translated by *would* or *should*.

23   **non dico Atheniensium**: *I don't mean (the state) of Athens.* Latin uses the name of the people rather than of the place. Athens, Carthage and Rhodes had all been strong naval powers in the past.

26   **usque ad nostram memoriam**: *right up to our time.*

27   **remansit**: Although singular, this verb has two subjects – **disciplina** and **gloria**.
    quae civitas, inquam, antea: After the long digression, Cicero repeats the opening words of his question.

29   **quae ... non defenderet**: For the use of the relative to introduce a Result Clause see page 32, line 24.

31   **legem Gabiniam**: The Lex Gabinia gave Pompey unprecedented powers in order to clear the Mediterranean of pirates once and for all. He completed his task in less than a year.

quodsi Romae Cn. Pompeius privatus esset hoc tempore,
tamen ad tantum bellum is erat deligendus atque
mittendus. nunc cum ad ceteras summas utilitates haec
quoque opportunitas adiungatur ut in iis ipsis locis adsit, ut
5 habeat exercitum, ut ab iis qui habent accipere statim possit,
quid exspectamus?

Catulus and Hortensius are opposed to Pompey's appointment. (a)
Hortensius is reluctant to hand over such a command to one man. He
had said that once before, but fortunately the Roman people did not take
his advice on that occasion. Pompey, in fact, was given the command
and has now freed the state from the threat of piracy.

at enim vir clarissimus, amantissimus rei publicae, vestris
beneficiis amplissimis affectus, Q. Catulus, itemque summis
ornamentis honoris, fortunae, virtutis, ingenii praeditus, Q.
10 Hortensius, ab hac ratione dissentiunt. quid igitur ait
Hortensius? si uni omnia tribuenda sint, dignissimum esse
Pompeium, sed ad unum tamen omnia deferri non
oportere. obsolevit iam ista oratio, re multo magis quam
verbis refutata. nam tu idem, Q. Hortensi, multa in senatu
15 contra virum fortem, A. Gabinium, graviter ornateque
dixisti, cum is de uno imperatore contra praedones
constituendo legem promulgasset, et ex hoc ipso loco
permulta item contra eam legem verba fecisti. quid?
tum, per deos immortales, si plus apud populum Romanum
20 auctoritas tua quam ipsius populi Romani salus valuisset,
hodie hanc gloriam atque hoc orbis terrae imperium
teneremus?
quae civitas antea umquam – non dico Atheniensium,
quae satis late quondam mare tenuisse dicitur, non
25 Carthaginiensium, qui permultum classe ac maritimis rebus
valuerunt, non Rhodiorum, quorum usque ad nostram
memoriam disciplina navalis et gloria remansit – quae
civitas, inquam, antea tam tenuis, quae insula tam parva fuit,
quae non portus suos et agros et aliquam partem regionis
30 atque orae maritimae per se ipsa defenderet? at hercle
aliquot annos continuos ante legem Gabiniam ille populus
Romanus, cuius ad nostram memoriam nomen invictum in
navalibus pugnis permanserit, magna parte non modo
utilitatis sed dignitatis atque imperii caruit. nos, quorum

1   **Antiochum**: This was Antiochus III of Syria, who gave asylum to Hannibal after the latter fled from Carthage. Antiochus was defeated by the Romans in a land battle at Magnesia in Asia (187 B.C.) and in two naval battles.

    Persem: Perses was the last king of Macedonia. He was beaten by the Romans in the land battle at Pydna (168 B.C.) and later captured by the commander of the Roman fleet.

3   **ii**: Translate as *we, I say*, since **ii** refers to **nos**.

6   **socios ... salvos praestare**: *to guarantee the safety of our allies*.

7   **idem**: *we, I repeat*. (Cf. **ii** in line 3.)

8   **Appia via**: The pirates became so daring that they even raided the west coast of Italy and kidnapped some officials who were travelling along the Via Appia, the main road south of Rome. (See page 24, line 7.)

9   **non pudebat magistratus**: *magistrates were not ashamed (to)*.

10   **hunc ipsum locum**: Once again, Cicero refers to the Speakers' Platform which was decorated with the prows (**rostra**) of ships captured in a naval battle against Antium (338 B.C.).

    eum: refers to **locum**.

12   **bono animo**: *with good intentions*.

    te ... et ceteros: Both of these accusatives are subjects of the infinitive **dicere**.

13   **erant in eadem sententia**: *were of the same opinion*, i.e. *agreed with you*.

14   **in salute communi**: *on (a matter concerning) the safety of the entire state*.

16   **una lex**: i.e. the Lex Gabinia.

18   **vere videremur ... imperare**: *we were really seen to be in control*.

22   **si quid eo factum esset**: *and (if) anything happened to him*.

23   **cepit ...... dignitatis**: *he received the great tribute which his high principles and status deserved*.

27   **in hoc ipso ... quod**: For this use of **hoc** compare page 32, line 23.

28   **quo minus certa ... hoc magis**: *the less certain ... the more*.

31   **at enim**: Having dealt with the first objection from Catulus, Cicero now quotes Catulus' second objection before attacking it. (cf. page 34, line 7.)

    ne quid novi fiat: literally *let nothing new be done*.

32   **in ipso Cn. Pompeio**: *in (the case of) Gnaeus Pompey himself* (cf. line 14 above and page 16, line 10). **ipso** here, as frequently, refers to what is currently under discussion.

33   **nova**: *innovations*, continues the idea contained in **quid novi** and **nihil novi**.

    summa ... voluntate: *with the full approval*.

maiores Antiochum regem classe Persemque superarunt
omnibusque navalibus pugnis Carthaginienses, homines in
maritimis rebus exercitatissimos paratissimosque, vicerunt, ii
nullo in loco iam praedonibus pares esse poteramus. nos,
5 qui antea non modo Italiam tutam habebamus sed omnes
socios in ultimis oris auctoritate nostri imperii salvos
praestare poteramus, idem non modo provinciis atque oris
Italiae maritimis ac portibus nostris sed etiam Appia iam via
carebamus. et iis temporibus non pudebat magistratus
10 populi Romani in hunc ipsum locum escendere, cum eum
nobis maiores nostri exuviis nauticis et classium spoliis
ornatum reliquissent! bono te animo tum, Q. Hortensi,
populus Romanus et ceteros, qui erant in eadem sententia,
dicere existimavit ea quae sentiebatis. sed tamen in salute
15 communi idem populus Romanus dolori suo maluit quam
auctoritati vestrae obtemperare. itaque una lex, unus vir,
unus annus non modo nos illa miseria ac turpitudine liberavit
sed etiam effecit ut aliquando vere videremur omnibus
gentibus ac nationibus terra marique imperare.

(*b*) *Catulus produces two main arguments against Pompey's
appointment : 'It is dangerous to stake everything on one man' and
'Nothing should be done which violates tradition'. Nevertheless,
Catulus has previously approved of precedents set in Pompey's case.*

20   reliquum est ut de Q. Catuli auctoritate et sententia
dicendum esse videatur. qui cum ex vobis quaereret, si in
uno Cn. Pompeio omnia poneretis, si quid eo factum esset, in
quo spem essetis habituri, cepit magnum suae virtutis
fructum ac dignitatis, cum omnes una prope voce in eo ipso
25 vos spem habituros esse dixistis. etenim talis est vir ut nulla
res tanta sit ac tam difficilis quam ille non et consilio regere et
integritate tueri et virtute conficere possit. sed in hoc ipso
ab eo vehementissime dissentio quod, quo minus certa est
hominum ac minus diuturna vita, hoc magis res publica,
30 dum per deos immortales licet, frui debet summi viri vita
atque virtute. at enim 'ne quid novi fiat contra exempla
atque instituta maiorum'. in ipso Cn. Pompeio, in quo nihil
novi constitui vult Q. Catulus, quam multa sint nova summa
Q. Catuli voluntate constituta, recordamini. quid tam

1 **adulescentulum privatum**: *a mere youth holding no office in the state.* Normally, an army could be raised only by a senior magistrate.

quid tam novum quam adulescentulum exercitum ... conficere: *what was so unprecedented as that a mere youth should raise an army.* With the two infinitives which follow (**praeesse** and **gerere**) understand **quid tam novum quam adulescentulum privatum**.

6 **bellum ... administrandum**: *the conduct of the war.*

provincia: This refers to the whole 'area of his responsibility' (i.e. both Sicily and Africa). In the next line **provinciis** refers to the individual 'provinces' of Sicily and Africa.

7 **innocentia, gravitate, virtute**: For this use of the ablative case with **esse** compare page 26, line 10.

8 **bellum in Africa**: Pompey was employed by Sulla to crush a Marian revolt in Sicily and Africa (82 B.C.). (See illustration on page 27.) Pompey was only twenty-four years old at the time.

victorem exercitum deportavit: *he (Pompey) brought his army home victorious.*

9 **equitem Romanum triumphare**: To the Romans this phrase would be a contradiction in terms. The right to hold a triumph was legally confined to senators holding the highest offices in the state. Pompey was only an **eques** and, at twenty-four, still too young to gain admission to the senate through even the lowest office, namely the quaestorship, for which the minimum qualifying age was thirty.

14 **in hoc bello Asiatico et regio**: *in this war waged in Asia against the power of kings.*

18 **propter eorum ... libidines et iniurias**: *because of the acts of lust and injustice of those ....*

19 **quod fanum ... religiosum ... fuisse**: Note that in this sentence there are three parts to Cicero's question, and **fuisse** has to be taken with all three, i.e. with **religiosum** and **sanctam** as well as with **clausam ac munitam.**

22 **quibus causa belli ... inferatur**: The phrase **bellum inferre** (+ dat.) means *to wage war (on)*. Cicero here combines the idea with **causa belli** (*pretext for war*) to suggest that they are looking for excuses to go to war against rich cities.

23 **libenter ... disputarem**: *I would gladly discuss* (i.e. if it were possible). This is really a conditional sentence in which the 'if' clause is assumed rather than stated. For the translation *would* compare page 34, line 19.

27 **hostium simulatione**: *under the pretence of attacking an enemy.*

novum quam adulescentulum privatum exercitum difficili rei
publicae tempore conficere?   confecit.   huic praeesse?
praefuit.   rem optime ductu suo gerere?   gessit.   quid tam
praeter consuetudinem quam homini peradulescenti
5 imperium atque exercitum dari, Siciliam permitti atque
Africam bellumque in ea provincia administrandum?   fuit
in his provinciis singulari innocentia, gravitate, virtute;
bellum in Africa maximum confecit, victorem exercitum
deportavit.   quid vero tam inauditum quam equitem
10 Romanum triumphare?   quid tam inusitatum quam ut,
cum duo consules clarissimi fortissimique essent, eques
Romanus ad bellum maximum formidolosissimumque pro
consule mitteretur?   missus est.

*He returns to the theme that Pompey is the ideal choice and strengthens
his argument by contrasting him with previous proconsuls who made
Rome detested locally because of their greed.*

atque in hoc bello Asiatico et regio non solum militaris illa
15 virtus, quae est in Cn. Pompeio singularis, sed aliae quoque
virtutes animi magnae et multae requiruntur.   difficile est
dictu, Quirites, quanto in odio simus apud exteras nationes
propter eorum, quos ad eas per hos annos cum imperio
misimus, libidines et iniurias.   quod enim fanum putatis in
20 illis terris nostris magistratibus religiosum, quam civitatem
sanctam, quam domum satis clausam ac munitam fuisse?
urbes iam locupletes et copiosae requiruntur quibus causa
belli propter diripiendi cupiditatem inferatur.   libenter haec
coram cum Q. Catulo et Q. Hortensio, summis et clarissimis
25 viris, disputarem.   noverunt enim sociorum vulnera, vident
eorum calamitates, querimonias audiunt.   pro sociis vos
contra hostes exercitum mittere putatis an hostium
simulatione contra socios atque amicos?   quae civitas est in

1   **non modo ...... militum**: Any Roman officer travelling through a province was entitled to a reception in keeping with his rank. The hospitality had to be extended also to junior officers such as the military tribune.

2   **animos ac spiritus capere possit**: *can put up with the acts of arrogance and insolence*. (Cf. page 38, line 18.)

3   **quem**: *someone*. After **si** and its compounds, **quis** usually means *someone or anyone*.

4   **nisi erit idem qui**: *unless he is also the sort of man who*.

11   **dubitare quin**: Compare page 32, line 31.

16   **auctore populo Romano**: *with the full backing of the Roman people*. Cicero is not unaware of the value of some obvious appeal to nationalist spirit, and he reserves it for his peroration.

18   **primum in te ...**: This **primum** refers to **primum** in line 14, *as for the first point*. Similarly, in line 19, translate **deinde** *on the second point*.

20   **cum tanto studio**: *showing such enthusiasm*.
   quid est quod: *why*.

22   **quicquid est ...... ingenii, id omne ... polliceor**: *whatever zeal, wisdom, energy or talent I possess, all of it I promise*. These genitives (called 'partitive genitives') are common after **quicquid**, **satis**, **nimis**, **plus**, **tantum**, etc. (e.g. **satis animi** in line 18 above, and **hoc tantum boni** in page 33, line 31).

24   **mihi susceptum est**: *has been undertaken by me*.

26   **tantum abest ut ... videar, ut ... intellegam**: *so far from seeming ... , I am aware ...*

29   **vobis non inutiles**: The double negative, *not useless*, produces a strong positive. Translate *vital for your sake*.
   ego me ... statui ... oportere: *I have decided that I ought*.
   hoc honore praeditum: *invested with this high office* (i.e. the praetorship)

30   **tantis ...... affectum**: *enjoying the great favours you have conferred on me*. Cicero took special pride in the fact that he had advanced so far through the **cursus honorum** in spite of the fact that he was not of noble birth.

31   **et ... et ... atque ...**: **atque** joins more closely than does **et** to the preceding word, phrase or statement. The provinces and the allies are clearly thought of together.

Asia, quae non modo imperatoris aut legati sed unius tribuni
militum animos ac spiritus capere possit? quare, etiamsi
quem habetis qui collatis signis exercitus regios superare
posse videatur, tamen, nisi erit idem qui se a pecuniis
5   sociorum, qui ab eorum coniugibus ac liberis, qui ab
ornamentis fanorum atque oppidorum, qui ab auro gazaque
regia manus, oculos, animum cohibere possit, non erit
idoneus qui ad bellum Asiaticum regiumque mittatur. ora
maritima, Quirites, Cn. Pompeium non solum propter rei
10 militaris gloriam sed etiam propter animi continentiam
requisivit. quare nolite dubitare quin huic uni credatis
omnia, qui inter tot annos unus inventus sit quem socii in
urbes suas cum exercitu venisse gaudeant.

*In conclusion, Cicero urges Manilius to continue to press forward with
his proposal to give the command to Pompey, and he states that he has
no ulterior motive in promising his own support.*

quae cum ita sint, C. Manili, primum istam tuam et legem
15 et voluntatem et sententiam laudo vehementissimeque
comprobo. deinde te hortor ut auctore populo Romano
maneas in sententia neve cuiusquam vim aut minas
pertimescas. primum in te satis esse animi
perseverantiaeque arbitror. deinde, cum tantam
20 multitudinem cum tanto studio adesse videamus, quid est
quod aut de re aut de perficiendi facultate dubitemus? ego
autem, quicquid est in me studii, consilii, laboris, ingenii, id
omne ad hanc rem conficiendam tibi ac populo Romano
polliceor ac defero. quicquid in hac causa mihi susceptum
25 est, Quirites, id ego omne me rei publicae causa suscepisse
confirmo. tantumque abest ut aliquam mihi bonam
gratiam quaesisse videar, ut multas me etiam simultates
partim obscuras, partim apertas intellegam mihi non
necessarias, vobis non inutiles suscepisse. sed ego me hoc
30 honore praeditum, tantis vestris beneficiis affectum statui,
Quirites, vestram voluntatem et rei publicae dignitatem et
salutem provinciarum atque sociorum meis omnibus
commodis et rationibus praeferre oportere.

EPILOGUE

Cicero had little difficulty in winning approval for the bill proposed by Manilius. There was, in fact, no one else who matched Pompey in experience, qualifications and past record of good fortune, a matter important to both Greeks and Romans.

As soon as he learned of his appointment under the Manilian Law, Pompey took over the military command from Lucullus. The latter had virtually broken the power of Mithridates by his succession of victories, but Mithridates had so far avoided final defeat.

Pompey gained an alliance with the Parthians, from whom Mithridates could now no longer expect aid. By careful disposition of his naval forces he cut Mithridates off from effective communication by sea, and it was not long before Mithridates sued for peace. Pompey was determined not to make peace without first securing a signal and well-publicised victory. Although the king had 30,000 infantry and 3,000 cavalry, he was unwilling to meet Pompey in pitched battle, and he was successful in avoiding such an encounter for a considerable time. At last, however, he was victim of a surprise attack from Pompey in Lesser Armenia and lost the greater part of his forces. Unable to obtain political asylum from Tigranes, he took refuge in his most distant dominion in the Cimmerian Bosporus.

Rather than pursue the fugitive, Pompey decided to attack Tigranes and, with the support of Tigranes' own son, he annexed Armenia without opposition. Tigranes offered to surrender, but Pompey generously acknowledged his kingship of Armenia and demanded only a payment of 6,000 talents. It was also agreed that Syria, Phoenicia, Cilicia and Cappadocia, all conquered by Lucullus, would belong to Rome. Having settled this, Pompey made Pontus a Roman province.

Meanwhile, Mithridates had been using his time to prepare for an open renewal of the contest, but he was prevented by a long illness from implementing his plans. Disaffection had arisen among his troops during his illness and this broke out into open insurrection, led by his own son. Forced to choose between death and captivity, he decided to take the poison which latterly he had constantly carried with him.

As for Pompey, his task and his self-justification were completed by his 'organisation of the East'. What had been a number of 'protectorates' now became a group of provinces under direct rule from Rome. He returned to Italy with his army at the end of 62 B.C. and duly disbanded his troops.

ADDITIONAL NOTES

p.8   **vectigalia**: One of the main business interests of the knights (**equites**) was the collection of taxes. The Romans did not have a system of taxation administered by the state, like our Inland Revenue or Customs and Excise. Instead, they put up for auction the right to collect taxes, and companies run by the **equites** made bids for these contracts. When a company made a successful bid, it agreed to hand over a lump sum to the Roman government. In making its offer, the company was gambling that it would recover this money and also make a profit from the taxes it collected in the province in question.

The main tax was the tithe (**decuma**), i.e. a tenth of the produce of each year. The amount that a company could collect was therefore largely dependent on the harvest. As the contract lasted five years, companies could, in normal circumstances, hope to balance years of bad harvest against years of good harvest, but constant raiding by Mithridates seriously threatened the security of their investments.

For details of different types of tax see page 14.

p.32 **Maximus, Marcellus, Scipio, Marius.** These were four of the great Roman consuls to whom the command of the army had been entrusted again and again. Q. Fabius Maximus was consul five times. It was he who successfully used delaying tactics against Hannibal in Italy and so earned the **cognomen** 'Cunctator'. M. Claudius Marcellus also was consul five times. He had considerable success in Sicily in the Second Punic War. P. Cornelius Scipio Aemilianus was consul only twice, but among his achievements was the final and total destruction of Carthage in 146 B.C. C. Marius was consul seven times. He ended the war against Jugurtha in North Africa in 106 B.C. and, four years later, repulsed an invasion of Germanic tribes in the north of Italy.

The Mediterranean area

This map shows the entire Mediterranean area as it was at the time when Cicero delivered his speech. It includes all the countries, territories and towns mentioned in the speech.

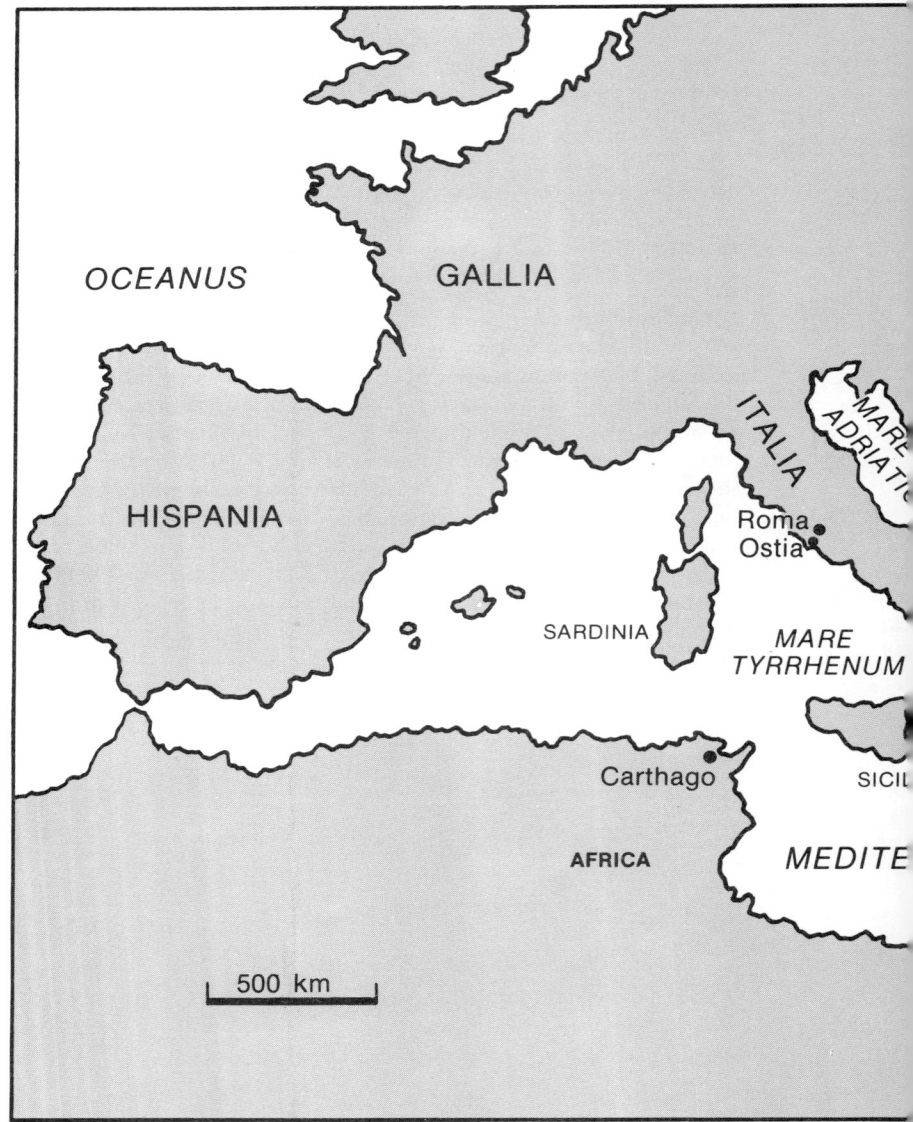

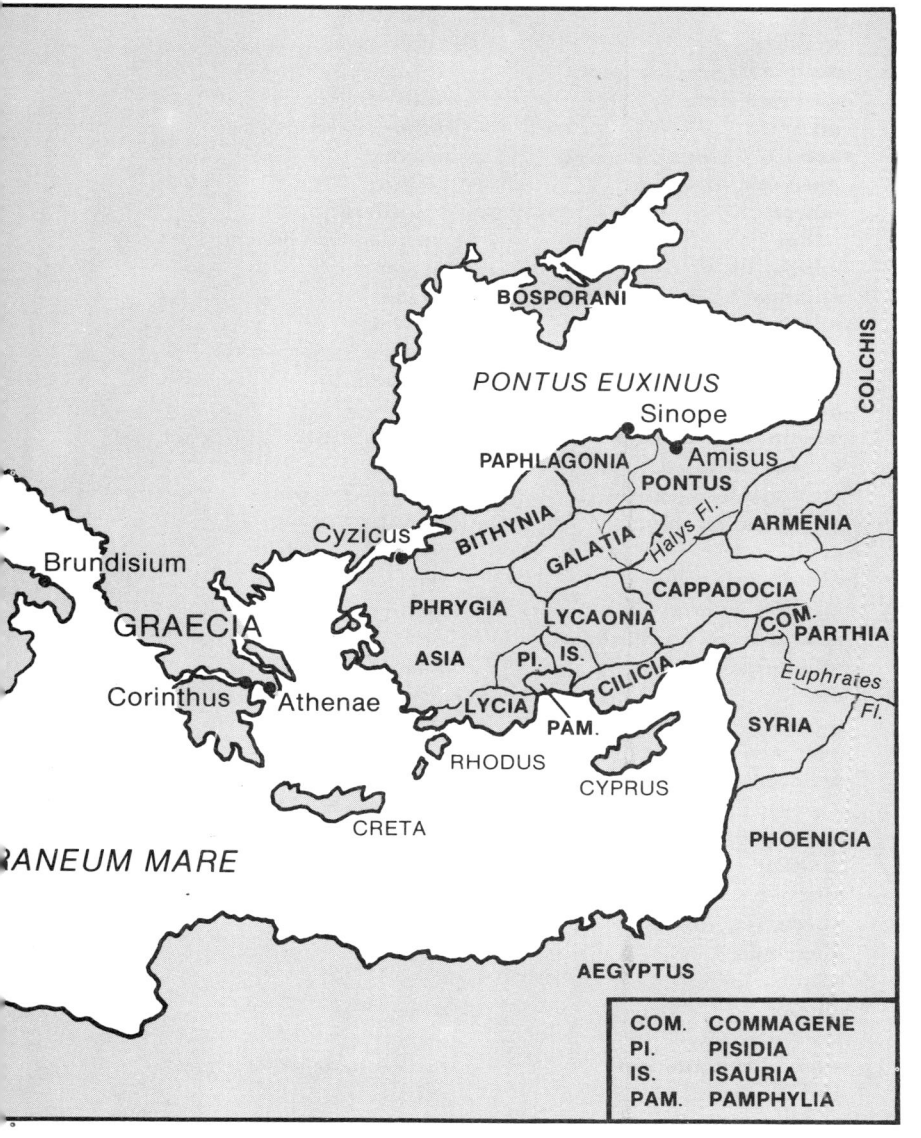

BOSPORANI

PONTUS EUXINUS

COLCHIS

Sinope

PAPHLAGONIA

Amisus

PONTUS

Halys Fl.

ARMENIA

Cyzicus

BITHYNIA

GALATIA

Brundisium

CAPPADOCIA

PHRYGIA

LYCAONIA

COM.

PARTHIA

GRAECIA

ASIA

PI.

IS.

Euphrates

Corinthus

Athenae

LYCIA

CILICIA

Fl.

RHODUS

PAM.

SYRIA

CYPRUS

CRETA

PHOENICIA

RANEUM MARE

AEGYPTUS

COM.	COMMAGENE
PI.	PISIDIA
IS.	ISAURIA
PAM.	PAMPHYLIA

VOCABULARY

Proper names are not listed if they appear in a map or a note.

A **a, ab** (+*abl.*) by, from
abditus, -a, -um hidden, secluded
absum, abesse, afui to be away
ac and, and also
accidit (it) happened
accipio (3), **-cepi, -ceptum** to receive, suffer
accuratissime with extreme care
ad (+*acc.*) to, for, (confer) upon
adduco (3), **-duxi, -ductum** to bring
adeo, -ire, -ii, -itum to go to
adfero See **affero**
adhuc up to this time, hitherto
aditus, -us (*m*) approach
adiungo (3), **-iunxi,-iunctum** to add
administro (1) to conduct
admurmuratio, -onis (*f*) murmur (of disapproval)
adorno (1) to provide
adsentio (4), **-sensi, -sensum** to agree
adsum, adesse, adfui to be there, be present, be at hand
adulescentia, -ae (*f*) youth
adventicius, -a, -um foreign
adventus, -us (*m*) arrival
aedifico (1) to build
aestas, -atis (*f*) summer
affectus, -a, -um honoured
affero, -ferre, attuli, allatum to bring, cite
afflictus, -a, -um ruined
age! well now! (used when moving from one section of the speech to another)

ager, agri (*m*) land, countryside
agitatus, -a, -um stirred up, restless
agnosco (3), **agnovi, agnitum** to recognise
ago (3), **egi, actum** to act, discuss, do
   agitur there is at stake
ait (he) says
alienus, -a, -um of someone else
aliquando at last
aliquis, -quid some, someone
aliquot some
alius, alia, aliud another, other
alter, altera, alterum the one, the other
amans patriae patriotic
amicus, -i (*m*) friend
amitto (3), **-misi, -missum** to lose

amplifico (1)	to enhance the greatness of
amplus, -a, -um	great
an	or
animus, -i (*m*)	mind, courage, attitude
annus, -i (*m*)	year
ante (+*acc.*)	before, in front of
ante (*adverb*)	earlier
antea	before, formerly
antecello (3)	to surpass
apertus, -a, -um	open, undisguised
apparo (1)	to prepare for
appello (1)	to address
appetens, -entis	eager for
apud (+*acc.*)	among, with
arbitror (1)	to think, consider
argentum, -i (*n*)	silver
arma, -orum (*n.pl*)	arms, weapons
ars, artis (*f*)	quality, skill
assiduitas, -atis (*f*)	perseverance
at	but
atque	and, and indeed, and also
auctoritas, -atis (*f*)	authority, prestige
audeo (2)**, ausus sum**	to dare
audio (4)**, -ivi, -itum**	to hear
aufero, -ferre, abstuli, ablatum	to carry off
auris, -is (*f*)	ear
aurum, -i (*n*)	gold
aut	either, or
autem	however, yet, moreover
auxilium, -i (*n*)	assistance
auxilia, -orum (*n.pl*)	auxiliary troops
avaritia, -ae (*f*)	greed
B **barbarus, -a, -um**	barbarian, foreign
bello (1)	to wage war
bellum, -i (*n*)	war
bene	well, successfully
beneficium, -i (*n*)	favour
bini, -orum	two
bona, -orum (*n.pl*)	property
bonus, -a, -um	good
Bosporani, -orum (*m.pl*)	inhabitants of the Cimmerian Bosporus
brevis, -is, -e	short
breviter	briefly
C **caelum, -i** (*n*)	heaven
calamitas, -atis (*f*)	disaster, ruin
capio (3)**, cepi, captum**	to take, capture, reap

careo (2), **-ui, -itum** (+*abl.*)	to lack, be unable to use
caritas, -atis (*f*)	high price
causa, -ae (*f*)	cause, case, position
causa (+*gen.*)	for the sake of
celeritas, -atis (*f*)	speed
celeriter	quickly
certe	assuredly
certus, -a, -um	certain, assured
ceteri, -ae, -a	the other(s), all other(s)
cingo (3), **cinxi, cinctum**	to surround, beset
civis, -is (*m*)	citizen
civitas, -atis (*f*)	state, city-state
clarus, -a, -um	outstanding, famous
classis, -is (*f*)	fleet
clausus, -a, -um	closed, secured
coepi, -isse, coeptum	I began, have begun
cogo (3), **coegi, coactum**	to compel
cognitio, -onis (*f*)	sight-seeing
cognosco (3), **-novi, -nitum**	to learn, discover
cohibeo (2), **-ui, -itum**	to keep from
collatis signis	in pitched battle
colligo (3), **-legi, -lectum**	to collect
commemoro (1)	to mention
committo (3), **-misi, -missum**	to expose, entrust
commodum, -i (*n*)	profit
commoveo (2), **-movi, -motum**	to affect
comparatio, -onis (*f*)	preparation
comparo (1)	to collect
complures, -es, -a or **-ia**	several
comprobo (1)	to approve
concerto (1)	to have a dispute with
concido (3), **-cidi**	to collapse
concipio (3), **-cepi, -ceptum**	to incur
concito (1)	to rouse
concupisco (3), **-ivi, -itum**	to aspire to
confero, -ferre, -tuli, collatum	to devote
se conferre	to turn to
conficio (3), **-feci, -fectum**	to complete, bring to an end, raise (an army)
confirmo (1)	to establish, strengthen, give courage to, declare
confiteor (2), **-fessus sum**	to acknowledge
confligo (3), **-flixi, -flictum**	to engage in combat with
coniectura, -ae (*f*)	guess
coniungo (3), **-iunxi, -iunctum**	to join
coniunx, coniugis (*f*)	wife
conquiesco (3), **-quievi, -quietum**	to cease
consequor (3), **consecutus sum**	to follow
conservo (1)	to keep, preserve

considero (1)	to consider, reflect
consilium, -i (*n*)	plan, strategy, wisdom
conspicio (3), **-spexi, -spectum**	to observe
constituo (3), **-ui, -utum**	to decide, appoint, establish (a precedent)
consuetudo, -inis (*f*)	custom
consul, consulis (*m*)	consul
consularis, -is (*m*)	an ex-consul
consulto	deliberately
contendo (3), **-tendi, -tentum**	to fight
contentus, -a, -um	satisfied
continentia, -ae (*f*)	self-control, restraint
contineo (2), **-ui, -tentum**	to restrain
continuus, -a, -um	successive
contra (+ *acc.*)	against, contrary to
copia, -ae (*f*)	abundance, subject matter
copiae, -arum (*f.pl*)	forces
copiosus, -a, -um	rich
coram	publicly
cotidie	every day
credo (3), **credidi, creditum**	to believe, entrust
culpa, -ae (*f*)	fault
cultura, -ae (*f*)	cultivation
cum (+ *abl.*)	with
cum (*conjunction*)	when, after, since, although
cunctus, -a, -um	the whole of
cupiditas, -atis (*f*)	(passionate) desire
cursus, -us (*m*)	course, voyage
D **de** (+ *abl.*)	about, down from
debeo (2), **-ui, -itum**	to owe, ought
declaro (1)	to proclaim
dedo (3), **dedidi, deditum**	to surrender, hand over
defendo (3), **defendi, defensum**	to defend
defero, -ferre, -tuli, -latum	to bring, confer upon, place at the disposal of
deinde	then, next, secondly
delabor (3), **-lapsus sum**	to descend
deleo (2), **-evi, -etum**	to destroy, wipe out
deliberatio, -onis (*f*)	consideration
deligo (3), **-legi, -lectum**	to choose, select
denique	in short, lastly, at last
depello (3), **-puli, -pulsum**	to avert
deposco (3), **deposci**	to demand
deprimo (3), **-pressi, -pressum**	to sink
depromo (3), **-prompsi, -promptum**	to draw out
desero (3), **-ui, -sertum**	to desert, abandon

desum, deesse, defui	to be lacking
detrimentum, -i (*n*)	loss, damage
detuli	See **defero**
deus, -i (*m*)	god
devoco (1)	to divert
dico (3)**, dixi, dictum**	to speak, say
difficile dictu	difficult to say
dies, diei (*m/f*)	day
difficilis, -is, -e	difficult
dignitas, -atis (*f*)	greatness, glory
dignus, -a, -um (+*abl.*)	worthy of
diligenter	carefully
dimico (1)	to fight
dimitto (3)**, -misi, -missum**	to demobilise
diripio (3)**, -ripui, -reptum**	to plunder
discedo (3)**, -cessi, -cessum**	to depart
disciplina, -ae (*f*)	training, skill
discrimen, -inis (*n*)	danger, risk
disiunctus, -a, -um	separated
dispersus, -a, -um	scattered
disputo (1)	to discuss
dissentio (4)**, -sensi, -sensum**	to disagree
dissipo (1)	to scatter
diuturnus, -a, -um	long-lasting
diversus, -a, -um	different
divido (3)**, divisi, divisum**	to divide
divinitus	by providence, sent by heaven
divinus, -a, -um	superhuman, inspired
divisus, -a, -um	extensive
do (1)**, dedi, datum**	to give, grant
dolor, -oris (*m*)	indignation, grief
domicilium, -i (*n*)	home, residence
domus, -us (*f*)	home
dubito (1)	to doubt, hesitate
dubius, -a, -um	doubtful
duco (3)**, duxi, ductum**	to lead, derive
ductus, -us (*m*)	leadership
dum	while, as long as
duo, duae, duo	two
duodecim	twelve
dux, ducis (*m*)	leader, general

E

e, ex (+*abl.*)	out of, from
efficio (3)**, -feci, -fectum**	to achieve
effecit ut . . .	brought it about that . . .
effugio (3)**, effugi**	to escape
egi	See **ago**
ego	I

egregius, -a, -um	outstanding
enim	for
eques, equitis (*m*)	knight
equitatus, -us (*m*)	cavalry
ereptus, -a, -um	taken away (violently)
erigo (3)**, erexi, erectum**	to comfort
erudio (4)	to train
escendo (3)**, escendi, escensum**	to climb, come up
et	and, even, also
et . . . et . . .	both . . . and . . .
etenim	for in fact
etiam	also, even
non modo . . . sed etiam . . .	not only . . . but also . . .
non solum . . . sed etiam . . .	not only . . . but also . . .
etiamsi	even if
excello (3)**, -ui, -celsum** (+ *dat.*)	to surpass
excipio (3)**, -cepi, -ceptum**	to welcome, offer asylum
excito (1)	to rouse
excruciatus, -a, -um	tortured
excursio, -onis (*f*)	raid
exemplum, -i (*n*)	example, precedent
exerceo (2)**, -ui, -itum**	to train, farm (taxes)
exercitatus, -a, -um	trained
exercitus, -us (*m*)	army
eximius, -a, -um	exceptional
existimo (1)	to consider, think
exitus, -us (*m*)	end, conclusion
exorsus, -us (*m*)	beginning, point of origin
expello (3)**, -puli, -pulsum**	to drive out
expeto (3)**, -petivi, -petitum**	to seek after
explico (1)	to rescue
exploro (1)	to reconnoitre
exporto (1)	to export
exspecto (1)	to look for, wait for
exstinctus, -a, -um	destroyed
exterus, -a, -um	foreign
extremus, -a, -um	the end of
extrema hieme	at the end of winter
extrema pueritia	at the end of his boyhood
exuro (3)**, -ussi, -ustum**	to burn down
exuviae, -arum (*f.pl*)	spoils, trophies
F facile	easily
facilitas, -atis (*f*)	accessibility
facio (3)**, feci, factum**	to do, make
facultas, -atis (*f*)	ability
fama, -ae (*f*)	report
familia, -ae (*f*)	staff

fanum, -i (*n*)	temple, shrine
felicitas, -atis (*f*)	luck, good fortune
fero, ferre, tuli, latum	to bear, endure
fertilis, -is, -e	fertile
fides, fidei (*f*)	credit, trustworthiness
finitimus, -a, -um	bordering on
finitimi, -orum (*m.pl*)	neighbours
firmus, -a, -um	strong
formido, -inis (*f*)	fear
formidolosus, -a, -um	frightening
fortasse	perhaps
fortis, -is, -e	brave, gallant
fortitudo, -inis (*f*)	courage
fortuna, -ae (*f*)	fortune (good or ill)
fortunae, -arum (*f.pl*)	wealth, fortunes
forum, -i (*n*)	the Forum
frater, fratris (*m*)	brother
fructus, -us (*m*)	crop, profit
frumentaria res	corn, grain
fruor (3), **fructus sum** (+*abl.*)	to reap the advantage (of)
fuga, -ae (*f*)	flight
fugio (3), **fugi, fugitum**	to flee, escape

G

Galli, -orum (*m.pl*)	Gauls
Gallia, -ae (*f*)	Gaul
gaudeo (2), **gavisus sum**	to be glad
gaza, -ae (*f*)	treasure
gens, gentis (*f*)	race, nation
genus, generis (*n*)	nature, kind
gero (3), **gessi, gestum**	to achieve
bellum gerere	to wage war
rem bene gerere	to achieve success
res gestae	achievements
gloria, -ae (*f*)	glory, fame, renown
Graeci, -orum (*m.pl*)	Greeks
gratia, -ae (*f*)	favour
gravis, -is, -e	serious, powerful
gravitas, -atis (*f*)	dignity
graviter	forcibly
guberno (1)	to navigate

H

habeo (2)	to have, keep
hercle!	upon my word!
hiberna, -orum (*n.pl*)	winter quarters
hic (*adverb*)	here
hic, haec, hoc	this; he, she, it
hiems, hiemis (*f*)	winter
Hispaniensis, -is, -e	Spanish

hodie	today
homo, hominis (*m*)	man; (plur.) men, people
honestus, -a, -um	honourable
hortor (1)	to urge
hostis, hostis (*m*)	enemy
humanitas, -atis (*f*)	humanity, civilised attitude

I

iam	now, already
idem, eadem, idem	same
tu idem	you also
idoneus, -a, -um	suitable, fit
igitur	therefore, then
ignoro (1)	not to know
ille, illa, illud	that; he, she, it
immineo (2)	to threaten
imminutus, -a, -um	reduced
immortalis, -is, -e	immortal
imperator, -oris (*m*)	general, commander
imperium, -i (*n*)	empire, command, power
impero (1)	to rule, command
impertio (4)	to bestow
impetus, -us (*m*)	attack
impudens, -entis	shameless
inauditus, -a, -um	unheard of
incipio (3), **-cepi, -ceptum**	to begin
incommodum, -i (*n*)	disaster
incredibilis, -is, -e	unbelievable, remarkable
incumbo (3), **-cubui, -cubitum**	to apply oneself to
inde	from that point, after that
industria, -ae (*f*)	energy
ineo, -ire, -ii, -itum	to begin
insum, -esse, infui	to be in
infero, -ferre, intuli, illatum	to introduce
bellum inferre (+ *dat.*)	to make war (upon)
inflammo (1)	to inflame
ingenium, -i (*n*)	ability, genius
ingratus, -a, -um	ungrateful
inicio (3), **-ieci, -iectum**	to inspire
inimicus, -a, -um	hostile
initium, -i (*n*)	beginning
innocens, -entis	upright, honest
innocentia, -ae (*f*)	integrity
insignia, -ium (*n.pl*)	emblems, symbols
insolitus, -a, -um	unaccustomed
instituo (3), **-ui, -utum**	to begin
institutum, -i (*n*)	custom
instruo (3), **-struxi, -structum**	to fit out
insula, -ae (*f*)	island

integer, integra, integrum	intact
integritas, -atis (*f*)	honesty
intellego (3), **-lexi, -lectum**	to understand
inter (+*acc.*)	during
interficio (3), **-feci, -fectum**	to kill
internicio, -onis (*f*)	massacre
intra (+*acc.*)	inside, within
intueor (2), **intuitus sum**	to look upon
inultus, -a, -um	unavenged
inusitatus, -a, -um	unusual
invenio (4), **-veni, -ventum**	to find
invictus, -a, -um	undefeated
invisus, -a, -um	hateful
ipse, ipsa, ipsum	himself, herself, myself, etc.
irascor (3), **iratus sum** (+*dat.*)	to be angry (with)
irruptio, -onis (*f*)	invasion
ita	so, in such a way
itaque	therefore
item	likewise
iter, itineris (*n*)	route, march
iudicium, -i (*n*)	judgement, decision
iussu (+*gen.*)	by order (of)
iuvo (1), **iuvi, iutum**	to help
in (+*abl.*)	in, on
in (+*acc.*)	into
is, ea, id	that; he, she, it
L **labefactus, -a, -um**	shaken, shattered
labor, -oris (*m*)	effort
lacesso (3), **-ivi, -itum**	to harass
laetitia, -ae (*f*)	joy
late	widely, far and wide
lateo (2)	to remain hidden
laudo (1)	to praise
laus, laudis (*f*)	praise
legatus, -i (*m*)	ambassador, second-in-command
legio, -onis (*f*)	legion
lego (3), **legi, lectum**	to read
lex, legis (*f*)	law
liber, libera, liberum	free
liberi, -orum (*m.pl*)	children
libero (1)	to set free
libertas, -atis (*f*)	freedom
libido, libidinis (*f*)	craving
licet (2)	it is permitted
litterae, -arum (*f.pl*)	letter, dispatch(es)
locuples, -etis	rich
locus, -i (*m*)	place

longe	far
longinquitas, -atis (*f*)	remoteness
ludus, -i (*m*)	school
lumen, luminis (*n*)	light
lux, lucis (*f*)	light

M

macula, -ae (*f*)	spot, stain
maeror, -oris (*m*)	grief
magis	more
magistratus, -us (*m*)	magistrate
magnitudo, -inis (*f*)	size, extent
magnus, -a, -um	great, large
maiores, -um (*m.pl*)	ancestors
malo, malle, malui	to prefer
malum, -i (*n*)	evil
mando (1)	to entrust
maneo (2), **mansi, mansum**	to remain
manere in sententia	to stand by one's opinion
manus, -us (*f*)	hand, army
mare, maris (*n*)	sea
maritimus, -a, -um	of the sea, at sea
maxime	especially
medius, -a, -um	the middle of
membrum, -i (*n*)	limb
mercator, -oris (*m*)	merchant
metuo (3), **-ui, -utum**	to fear
metus, -us (*m*)	fear
meus, -a, -um	my
miles, militis (*m*)	soldier
milia, milium (*n.pl*)	thousands
militaris, -is, -e	military, soldierly
ars militaris	the art of war
militia, -ae (*f*)	military service
militiae	on military service
minae, -arum (*f.pl*)	threats
minor (1)	to threaten
minus	less
miror (1)	to wonder
miseria, -ae (*f*)	distress
mitto (3), **misi, missum**	to send
modo	only
modus, -i (*m*)	limit
mors, mortis (*f*)	death
motus, -us (*m*)	movement
multi, -ae, -a	many
multitudo, -inis (*f*)	great number, crowd
multo	much
munio (4)	to strengthen, fortify

N nam — for

natio, -onis (*f*) — nation, people

nauticus, -a, -um — naval

navalis, -is, -e — naval

navigo (1) — to sail

navis, navis (*f*) — ship

ne — in case

ne . . . . . . quidem — not even

necessarius, -a, -um — necessary, inevitable

neco (1) — to kill

neglego (3), -lexi, -lectum — to neglect

negotium, -i (*n*) — undertaking

nemo — no one

neque — and not, nor

  neque . . . neque . . . — neither . . . nor . . .

neve — and not

nihil — nothing

nimius, -a, -um — excessive

nisi — unless, if not

noceo (2), -ui, -itum (+*dat.*) — to harm

nolite (+*inf.*) — do not . . . !

nomen, -inis (*n*) — name, fame, reputation

nomino (1) — to name

non — not

nondum — not yet

nonne? — surely? did . . . not?

nos — we, us

noster, nostra, nostrum — our

  nostri, -orum (*m.pl*) — our men

novi, novisse — to know

novus, -a, -um — new

nullus, -a, -um — no

num? — whether?

numerus, -i (*m*) — number

numquam — never

nunc — now

nuntius, -i (*m*) — messenger, message

nuper — lately

O oblatus — See **offero**

oblivio, -onis (*f*) — forgetting

oboedio (4) — to obey

obscurus, -a, -um — concealed

obsecundo (1) — to obey, comply

obsideo (2), -sedi, -sessum — to besiege

obsidio, -onis (*f*) — siege

obsolesco (3), -evi, -etum — to go out of date

obtempero (1) — to submit, comply (with)

occasio, -onis *(f)*	opportunity
occupatus, -a, -um	tied up, invested
oculus, -i *(m)*	eye
odium, -i *(n)*	hatred
in odio esse	to be hated
offensio, -onis *(f)*	reverse, disaster
offero, offerre, obtuli, oblatum	to offer, present
omnis, -is, -e	every, all
opimus, -a, -um	rich, fertile
opinio, -onis *(f)*	belief, conviction
oportet	must, ought
oppidum, -i *(n)*	town, municipality
opprimo (3), **-pressi, -pressum**	to crush, overwhelm
optime	very well
opto (1)	to hope for
ora, -ae *(f)*	region, coast
oratio, -onis *(f)*	speech, words
orbis terrae ⎫ **orbis terrarum** ⎭	the world
ornamentum, -i *(n)*	distinction, work of art
ornate	brilliantly
orno (1)	to decorate, fit out, equip

P par, paris	equal, a match (for)
paratus, -a, -um	prepared, equipped
parens, -entis *(m)*	father
pars, partis *(f)*	part, side, faction
aliqua ex parte	to some extent
partim	partly
partim . . . partim	some . . . others; either . . . or
parvus, -a, -um	small
pastio, -onis *(f)*	pasture-land
patefacio (3), **-feci, -factum**	to open up
pater, patris *(m)*	father; (plur.) ancestors
patior (3), **passus sum**	to allow, permit
patrius, -a, -um	of a father
pauca *(n.pl)*	a few words, briefly
paulo	a little
pax, pacis *(f)*	peace
pecunia, -ae *(f)*	money; (plur.) fortunes
pensito (1)	to pay
per (+ *acc.*)	through, during
per se	by its own power
per deos	in heaven's name
per deos licet	it is permitted by the gods
peradulescens, -entis	very young
perbrevis, -is, -e	very short
perditus, -a, -um	ruined, forlorn

perfectus, -a, -um	of consummate skill
perfero, -ferre, -tuli, -latum	to carry, convey across
perficio (3), **-feci, -fectum**	to accomplish, conclude successfully
periculosus, -a, -um	dangerous, perilous
periculum, -i (*n*)	danger, risk, menace
permagnus, -a, -um	very large, immense
permaneo (2), **-mansi, -mansum**	to remain
permulti, -ae, -a	very many
persequor (3), **-secutus sum**	to pursue, follow up
perseverantia, -ae (*f*)	determination
pertimesco (3), **-timui**	to fear greatly, shudder at
pertineo (2), **-tinui, -tentum**	to be relevant or important
pertuli	See **perfero**
pervado (3), **-vasi, -vasum**	to spread, spread through
pervenio (4), **-veni, -ventum**	to arrive, reach, come
plures, plures, plura	more
plurimi, -ae, -a	very many
plurimum posse	to be very strong
poena, -ae (*f*)	punishment
polliceor (2), **pollicitus sum**	to promise
pono (3), **posui, positum**	to place
populus, -i (*m*)	people
portus, -us (*m*)	harbour
possum, posse, potui	to be able, to be strong
postea	afterwards
posteaquam	after
postremo	finally
potens, potentis	powerful
potestas, -atis (*f*)	power, control
potissimum	especially
praeceptum, -i (*n*)	teaching, instruction
praeclarus, -a, -um	notable
praeda, -ae (*f*)	booty, plunder
praedico (1)	to proclaim
praeditus, -a, -um	endowed, invested (with)
praedo, -onis (*m*)	pirate
praefero, -ferre, -tuli, -latum	to regard as more important
praeficio (3), **-feci, -fectum** (+*dat.*)	to put in command (of)
praepono (3), **-posui, -positum** (+*dat.*)	to put in charge (of)
praesidium, -i (*n*)	garrison
praesto (1), **praestiti**	to guarantee, keep
praesum, praeesse, praefui (+*dat.*)	to be in command (of)
praeter (+*acc.*)	more than, beyond, contrary to
praeterea	besides
praetereo, -ire, -ii, -itum	to omit, gloss over
primum	firstly, in the first place

principium, -i (*n*)	beginning
privatus, -i (*m*)	private citizen (i.e. one not holding public office)
pro (+ *abl.*)	on behalf of, in defence of
pro di immortales!	O ye immortal gods!
proelium, -i (*n*)	battle
profecto	certainly, assuredly
proficiscor (3)**, profectus sum**	to set out, start, begin
profugio (3)**, -fugi**	to flee, escape
prohibeo (2)**, -ui, -itum**	to protect, preserve
promulgo (1)	to introduce (a law)
prope	nearby, almost
proprius, -a, -um	characteristic
propter (+ *acc.*)	on account of, because of
propter (*adverb*)	near at hand
propterea quod	because, for the simple reason that
propugnaculum, -i (*n*)	bulwark
prostratus, -a, -um	laid low, overthrown
provideo (2)**, -vidi, -visum**	to plan ahead, foresee
provincia, -ae (*f*)	province, command
publicanus, -i (*m*)	tax-gatherer
pueritia, -ae (*f*)	boyhood
extrema pueritia	at the end of his boyhood
pugna, -ae (*f*)	battle
pulcher, pulchra, pulchrum	beautiful
pulsus, -a, -um	defeated, worsted
puto (1)	to think, imagine, suppose

Q
qua	where
quaero (3)**, quaesivi, quaesitum**	to ask, look for
qualis, -is, -e	what sort of
quam!	how!
tam ... quam ...	as ... as ...
quam (+ *comparative*)	than
quamquam	although
quantus, -a, -um	how great
tantus ... quantus ...	as great as
quare	therefore; why
-que	and
quemadmodum	how
querimonia, -ae (*f*)	complaint
queror (3)**, questus sum**	to complain
qui, quae, quod	who, which; which?, what?
quicquid	whatever
quid?	again
quidam, quaedam, quoddam	a certain, some, a
quidem	See **ne ... quidem**
quies, quietis (*f*)	rest, respite

quis, quis, quid	anyone, anything; who? what?
quisquam, quidquam	anyone, anything
quod	because; the fact that ...
quondam	formerly, once
quoniam	since
quoque	also

R **ratio, rationis** (*f*)	method, system, argument, interest
recipio (3), **-cepi, -ceptum**	to take back
se recipere	to withdraw, return
recordor (1)	to think of, remember
recreo (1)	to revive, give new life to
redimo (3), **redemi, redemptum**	to buy back, ransom
redundo (1)	to overflow
refertus, -a, -um (+*gen.*)	full (of), filled (with)
refuto (1)	to disprove
regio, -onis (*f*)	land, area
regius, -a, -um	royal
regno (1)	to rule, reign
regnum, -i (*n*)	kingdom
rego (3), **rexi, rectum**	to rule, manage
religiosus, -a, -um	sacred, sacrosanct
relinquo (3), **-liqui, -lictum**	to leave behind, abandon, leave undone
reliquus, -a, -um	remaining, other, rest
reliquum est ut (+*subj.*)	it remains (for me) to ...
remaneo (2), **-mansi, -mansum**	to continue
remex, remigis (*m*)	oarsman
remoror (1)	to delay, hinder
repente	suddenly
reporto (1)	to carry off (as victor)
victoriam reportare	to win a victory
requiro (3), **-quisivi, -quisitum**	to ask for, earnestly seek
res, rei (*f*)	thing, affair
rem gerere	to conduct a campaign
res frumentaria	corn
res gestae	achievements
res maritimae	naval power, naval resources
res militaris	military skill, warfare
res publica	the republic, the state
restat ut (+*subj.*)	it remains to
retardo (1)	to slow down, delay
revoco (1)	to recall
rex, regis (*m*)	king, ruler
Rhodii, -orum (*m.pl*)	the people of Rhodes
rumor, -oris (*m*)	rumour, report
ruo (3), **rui, rutum**	to fall in ruins

S saepe — often
salus, -utis (*f*) — safety, well-being
salvus, -a, -um — safe, unharmed
sanctus, -a, -um — sacred, inviolable
sanguis, sanguinis (*m*) — blood
sapiens, sapientis — wise
satis — sufficiently, enough
scelus, sceleris (*n*) — crime
sciens, scientis — knowledgeable
scientia, -ae (*f*) — knowledge, expertise
se or sese — himself, herself, itself, themselves
  secum — along with them
secundus, -a, -um — successful
securis, -is (*f*) — axe
sed — but
semper — always
senatus, -us (*m*) — senate
sententia, -ae (*f*) — opinion, proposal
  in sententia manere — to stand by one's resolve
sentio (4), sensi, sensum — to feel
sermo, sermonis (*m*) — common talk, gossip
servilis, -is, -e — against slaves
servio (4) — to be subject to
servitus, -utis (*f*) — slavery
si — if
sic — in such a way, thus, in this way, like this
sicut — as
significatio, -onis (*f*) — communication
signum, -i (*n*) — statue, standard
simulatio, -onis (*f*) — pretence
simulo (1) — to pretend
simultas, -atis (*f*) — enmity
sine (+*abl.*) — without
singularis, -is, -e — remarkable, outstanding, unique
singuli, -ae, -a — individual, separate
sino (3), sivi, situm — to allow
Sinope, -es (*f*) — Sinope, a town in Paphlagonia
sinus, -us (*m*) — bay
socius, -i (*m*) — ally, friend
soleo (2), solitus sum — to be in the habit of
solum — only
solus, -a, -um — only, alone
spero (1) — to hope
spes, spei (*f*) — hope, expectation
spiritus, -us (*m*) — arrogance
splendor, -oris (*m*) — brilliance, lustre
spolium, -i (*n*) — spoil (of conquest)
statim — immediately

statuo (3), statui, statutum	to judge, decide
stipendium, -i (n)	campaign; (plur.) military service
studium, -i (n)	enthusiasm, zeal
subsidium, -i (n)	assistance; (plur.) resources
succedo (3), -cessi, -cessum (+dat.)	to take the place (of)
summus, -a, -um	greatest, outstanding, highest
summa hieme	in the depths of winter
superbe	arrogantly, disrespectfully
supero (1)	to defeat, surpass
suscipio (3), -cepi, -ceptum	to incur, adopt, undertake
suus, -a, -um	his, her, its, their (own)
T tabula, -ae (f)	picture, painting
tacitus, -a, -um	silent
talis, -is, -e	such, of such a kind, like this
tam	so, such, so much, as
tamen	but, nevertheless, still
tametsi	although, despite the fact that
tandem	(in questions) tell me, I ask you
tantum	only
tantus, -a, -um	such, so/as much, so/as great
tardo (1)	to delay
tectum, -i (n)	home
temperantia, -ae (f)	self-control
tempestas, -atis (f)	storm
tempestivus, -a, -um	fit, suitable
templum, -i (n)	temple
tempus, temporis (n)	time, occasion
teneo (2), -ui, tentum	to keep, hold, possess, control
tenuis, -is, -e	weak, insignificant
terra, -ae (f)	land, country
terra marique	by land and sea
orbis terrae/terrarum	the world
terror, -oris (m)	fear, alarm
tertius, -a, -um	third
testis, -is (m)	witness
timide	cautiously
tollo (3), sustuli, sublatum	to remove, take away
tot	so many, as many
totus, -a, -um	the whole of, entire
tracto (1)	to treat
trado (3), tradidi, traditum	to hand down, hand over
traho (3), traxi, tractum	to drag, draw
Transalpinus, -a, -um	Transalpine, in Transalpine Gaul
transmitto (3), -misi, -missum	to cross, cross over
tres, tres, tria	three
tribunus, -i (m)	tribune
tribunus militum	military tribune

tribuo (3), **-ui, -utum**	to bestow, ascribe, assign
triumpho (1)	to celebrate a triumph
triumphus, -i (*m*)	a triumph
tu	you (sing.)
tueor (2)	to secure, preserve
tuli	See **fero**
tum	then, at that time, on that occasion
turpis, -is, -e	shameful, inglorious
turpitudo, -inis (*f*)	shame, disgrace
tutor (1)	to protect
tutus, -a, -um	safe, secure
tuus, -a, -um	your, yours

U

ubertas, -atis (*f*)	fertility
ullus, -a, -um	any
ultimus, -a, -um	farthest, most remote
umquam	ever
unde	from where, from which
undequinquagesimus, -a, -um	forty-ninth
undique	on all sides
universus, -a, -um	taken collectively, entire
unus, -a, -um	one, a single, only
urbs, urbis (*f*)	city, town
usquam	anywhere
usque	all the way, right up (to)
usus, -us (*m*)	experience, practice
ut (+*indic.*)	as, when
ut (+*subj.*)	so that, in order that, that, to
utilitas, -atis (*f*)	usefulness, advantage
utinam	would that, I wish that
utor (3), **usus sum** (+*abl.*)	to use, enjoy
utrum ... an ... ?	(whether) ... or ... ?

V

valeo (2)	to be strong, be powerful, carry weight
varietas, -atis (*f*)	diversity
varius, -a, -um	different
vectigal, -alis (*n*)	tax, revenue
vectigalis, -is, -e	paying tax
vehemens, -entis	strong, powerful
vehementer	strongly, violently, heartily
venia, -ae (*f*)	pardon
venio (4), **veni, ventum**	to come, arrive
ventus, -i (*m*)	wind
ver, veris (*n*)	spring
verber, -eris (*n*)	flogging
verbum, -i (*n*)	word
verba facere	to speak, say
vero	however, indeed, in fact

verum tamen	but all the same, nonetheless
vester, vestra, vestrum	your
vestigium, -i (*n*)	mark, footprint
vetus, veteris	old, former
vicesimus, -a, -um	twentieth
victor, -oris (*m*)	victor, victorious
victoria, -ae (*f*)	victory
vicus, -i (*m*)	village
video (2)**, vidi, visum**	to see, consider
videor (2)**, visus sum**	to seem, appear
vinco (3)**, vici, victum**	to defeat, vanquish
vincula, -orum (*n.pl*)	chains, imprisonment
vir, viri (*m*)	man, hero
virtus, -utis (*f*)	merit, worth, excellence, good qualities, courage, virtue
vis, vim, vi (*f*)	quantity, power, violence
viso (3)**, visi, visum**	to look at
vita, -ae (*f*)	life
vix	scarcely
voco (1)	to call, draw, place, put
volo, velle, volui	to wish, want, be willing
voluntas, -atis (*f*)	wish, will, goodwill, approval
voluptas, -atis (*f*)	pleasure
vos	you (plur.)
vox, vocis (*f*)	voice
una voce	unanimously, with one accord
vulgo	commonly, generally
vulnus, -eris (*n*)	wound, misfortune